Lasting Matters

WRITERS 57 AND OVER . . .

Nimrod International Journal

Lasting Matters

WRITERS 57 AND OVER . . .

ISBN: 978-0-9860178-1-0   ISSN: 0029-053X
Volume 56, Number 2
Spring/Summer 2013

THE UNIVERSITY OF TULSA — TULSA, OKLAHOMA

This issue of Nimrod *is dedicated to*
Margery Mayo Feagin Bird,
1916-2012

*Margery Mayo Feagin Bird was a role model in her long
vivid life and in her example of giving, especially to
organizations supporting the arts and education. In her
eighties, Margery parasailed in Mexico, helicoptered in
the Caribbean and Yellowstone Park, ballooned in Africa,
and always drove her friends to lectures and social occasions.
Daring, modest, elegant Margery rarely missed a chance to
attend the* Nimrod *Awards dinner and delight in the newly
discovered writers she found there, or climb the stairs in her
house (a health practice we all might try to emulate). Now
she has helped* Nimrod *to climb into the future.*

Surrender

I never knew what to expect
when life left the body
that final shrug of the shoulders,
the letting go, the exit of the soul
when the spirit flies
out of the window to be with god,
or angels or some eternal dust.
Perhaps a bird, a majestic white bird
caught in the high draft
of a delicate breeze,
captured her spirit in his soul
and soared into the sun
over the rims of hills
just beyond the horizon
where love gathers the hungry
and heads home.

—Ann Zoller

ACKNOWLEDGEMENTS

This issue of *Nimrod* is funded by donations, subscriptions, and sales. *Nimrod* and The University of Tulsa acknowledge with gratitude the many individuals and organizations that support *Nimrod*'s publication, annual prize, and outreach programs: *Nimrod*'s Advisory and Editorial Boards; and *Nimrod*'s Angels, Benefactors, Donors, and Patrons.

ANGEL
($1,000+)

Ellen and Steve Adelson, Margery Bird, Ivy and Joseph Dempsey, Joan Flint, Stephani Franklin, Susan and Robert Mase, The Ruth K. Nelson Trust, Harry Potter, Ann Daniel Stone, Randi and Fred Wightman, The John Steele Zink Foundation

BENEFACTOR
($500+)

Bruce Kline, George Krumme, Lisa Ransom and David Flesher, Francine Ringold, The Kathleen Patton Westby Foundation, Jane Wiseman

DONOR
($100+)

Teresa and Alex Adwan, Harvey Blumenthal, Colleen Boucher, Kenneth Bruce, Jackie and Mark Darrah, Marion and William Elson, Nancy and Raymond Feldman, Ken Fergeson, Joann and Robert Franzen, Sherri Goodall, Cynthia Gustavson, Helen Jo Hardwick, Frank Henke III, Nancy and William Hermann, Linda Jennings, Carol Johnson, Elizabeth and Sam Joyner, The Kerr Foundation, David and Marjorie Kroll, Lydia Kronfeld, Robert LaFortune, Maria Lyda, Laura Maslon, Roberta Marder, Geraldine McLoud, Carol McGraw, Catherine Gammie Nielsen, Donna O'Rourke and Tom Twomey, Nancy and Thomas Payne, Pamela and Larry Pearce, Judy and Roger Randle, Dana Rasure and Roy Breedlove, Patricia and Gil Rohleder, Joan and Harry Seay, Diane and James Seebass, Dorothy and Michael Tramantana, Fran and Bruce Tibbetts, Renata and Sven Treitel, Melissa and Mark Weiss, Joy Whitman, Penny Williams, Josephine Winter, Mary Young and Joseph Gierek, Ann Zoller

PATRON
($50+)

Helen and M. E. Arnold, Mary Cantrell and Jason Brimer, Linda and William Epperson, Kimberly Doenges, Kay and Daniel Duffy, Britton Gildersleeve, William Kellough, Steve Liggett, Leslie and Chris Matthies, Connie Murray, Taylor and Joshua Parish, Glenda and Larry Silvey, Linda and Bruce Stoesser, Krista and John Waldron, Ann Watson, Ruth Weston, Patricia Wheeler, Martin Wing

TABLE OF CONTENTS

Editor's Note
Lasting Matters: Writers over 57

This issue, "Lasting Matters" (*Lasting* Matters or Lasting *Matters* wherever you choose to place the emphasis), though limited to writers over 57 (five are in their late 80's, one is 96), is boundless in content and spirit. Good words are always lasting, so are good people. They last in our memory and on the page. But why 57? Amazing as it may seem to those who know the typical history of "lit mags" (2 to 10 years at most), this fall 2013 *Nimrod International Journal* will be celebrating its 57th year of continuous publication. With the guidance and dedication of our advisory and editorial boards, *Nimrod* promises to last another 57 years or more.

Most important, however, to our decision to focus on mature writers and writing is that the so-called "boom" generation (ages 48-67), and seniors living into their 90's present a virtual new culture, a culture "on the edge." The precarious, the unsettled have always been a great source of creative energy, witness *Nimrod*'s Arabic, Chinese, Latin American, and Soviet issues, all published during the period when these lands and peoples were (and perhaps still are) undergoing revolutionary changes.

Now, if the poems and stories that follow are indicative, established writers—like former Poet Laureate Ted Kooser; Pulitzer prize-winning poet Stephen Dunn; Canada's winner of the Governor General's Award, Lorna Crozier; Slovenian author Tomaž Šalamun; and famed contemporary Russian poet Oleg Chukhontsev—never wanting to repeat themselves, are making a lively mark along with published writers 60, 70, 80 years old, and writers returning to their craft after years of involvement in other fields. On the edge, challenged by being sandwiched between aging children and parents, by early retirement and thinning wallets, these writers 57 and over (and their counterparts in art and even tap dancing, as with the Bert Chan Dancers in Santa Monica, California) often are not only living longer, healthier lives, but have been given the gift of expanding initial insights into wisdom, of having time and space to reach and risk beyond the humdrum and into vivid modes of expression.

Rest assured, this issue does not consist exclusively of fiction and poetry about aging. Neither sociologic tract, nor political statement, it ranges from Maimonides to the common life, from a passion for sports to a love of gardens and dogs, from travel to the pleasure of staying home, from the seasons on earth to the galaxy, from "rapture" and "sex at seventy" to emerging sexuality as in Vince Sgambati's story "What Took You So Long?" Politics, paintings, urban blight and urban vitality, rural tranquility and primal violence—all serve as inspiration, as a prompt to reach out and grab a pen or pound a keyboard. Age has no boundaries when it comes to subject matter, nor do complex thinking and deep considered feeling. If one expects mawkishness from writers 57 and over, one should think again. The works included in this issue are often filled with sentiment but not that excess of ungrounded feeling that is known as "sentimentality." Nor do cynics abound— a few curmudgeons, perhaps, but not cynics!

Selected from over 2,000 individual submissions, these poems and stories and memoirs are often tough, always reflect a depth of thought, a lively spirit, a willingness to find new forms and to refine traditional styles. Take Lilvia Soto's story "History for Ambassadors or Butterflies and Other Chingaderas," for example. The author is 80+, the style a modernist pastiche of fragments and subtle links, whereas Roberta Murphy's "Blue Skies" tells a story of division in a traditional mode spiced with irony and a Texas twang. Ron Wallace's series of poems, beginning with "Sex at Seventy" is a sonnet sequence in which the last word of each line, read vertically, from top to bottom, forms a haiku by Issa, Basho or Buson. Yet each of Wallace's sonnets is unique, fresh in content and the style with which it imprints experience.

Whether in an experimental or traditional mode, whether humorous or serious, these authors seem to be saying that lasting does matter, that here is life, with all its whims and complications, as I have experienced it but also as I have shaped it. Here are dreams and stones and other hard realities. Share them with me.

Lasting Matters

Todd Camp, *When It Happens to You*, acrylic, collage, and
encaustic on canvas, 12" x 12"

Shame

You were a college student, a waitress
paying your way through the 'sixties,
and I was recently divorced, alone
and lonely, looking for someone to love
in those dreary years when it seemed
no one else was willing "to make
a commitment," as we said back then,
and I mustered my courage and asked you
to dinner, and met you at your door,
and we walked downtown, both of us shy,
both awkward, both scented and scrubbed
and overdressed and clopping along
in new and uncomfortable shoes,
and over wine and dinner, as we began
to feel more comfortable together,
sometimes touching each other's hands,
I told you my story and you told me
yours, the way young people will,
you finishing yours with the news
that you had leukemia, the slow kind
that with "adequate treatment"
could keep you alive, at least for a time,
and it frightened me, having no courage
for anyone's pain but my own, knowing
nothing at all about love, and surely
you must have been terribly hurt
to read all that in my expression,
and forty years later I'm still ashamed
to have been the kind of person
who could then walk you back to your door
still early in the evening, and leave you
there with a dry little kiss and a promise,
who would never phone, who would avoid
the restaurant where I'd first seen you
wiping the tables, working your way
through so much more than college,
you in your starched uniform apron
with a plastic tag pinned to your breast
and your name that I've even forgotten.

Picking up after the Dead

This brother and sister have come from
hundreds of miles apart to sort through
the mold and clutter left in the wake
of their maiden aunt, who as the future
closed about her assembled a proof
of the past, heaped in the rooms
she'd played in as a child, her toys,
her picture books, piles of newspapers
nibbled by mice, and over the years
all of the black and white issues
of *Life* that arrived by subscription,
though life for her had already arrived
for free and in muted color, curtains
parted for peeks at the seasons —
their watery green, the browns, a white —
the bone-yellow ribs of bent lath
where the ceilings had fallen,
and in the parlor an upright piano,
dark orange-peel finish clouded
with mildew, and half of its keys
stuck down as if a tremendous chord
had been hammered into the silence
and had faded only a moment before
her niece's key rattled into the lock
and these two, who once had been children
visiting there, stepped cautiously into
the stinky kitchen where she'd been found
sprawled on the cracked linoleum
with history scattered around her,
even her one chipped, varnishy cup
there by the sink with the jar of Sanka.

Howard

Our old white lab lies on the stoop,
watching the pre-dawn darkness
stealing from tree to tree beyond him,
a slight disturbance in the light
like a flaw in a pane of glass,
and wary, too, this shape that keeps
its eyes on Howard, bright as a moon
under the porch light. And I'd guess
it probably knows that he can
smell it too, its ripply scent a cold
that floats on the rest of the cold
like a snake on a pool, and maybe
it thinks that this old sphinx
with his stiffening joints might still
be able, suddenly, to come to life
and chase and catch and kill
whatever he has a hunger for,
though he and I know different.

Wind Dog

What are you sniffing out there
nose pointed to the sky?
Leaves, crisp ochre and russet,
signal from the arms of the oak.
Caught in each gust,
they tumble to earth, and you
pile on with them,
jump into the middle and fly.

So the season of the fall begins
as it should, not with a long mournful wail
but a howl of delight,
welcoming squall and sun,
reminders of the passion
we set by for our long winter's nap.

This Morning

A weeping pipe, a peep.

Silence. Finally, a persistent whine
and again that urgent peep,
neither bird nor human.

The light is up, Pete with it.
He stretches . . . . Sighs.
Cocks his head.
Waits.
Does a star dance when I appear.

So it is with attachment. It feeds us.
It lets us bask in its sun.

Declan IV

I hold a photograph of you sitting in a box
Half-full of trim from the ancient pepper tree
Whose leaves would choke the eaves and drives and vex
The neighbor lady, who pleaded for the penalty

Of downing—this for a being much of her time.
She'd pass, pure white, beneath the "dirty" limbs.
"There's a fungus among us," my mom would chime
By way of warning. Indeed, there was. Death has her hymns.

But here you are, roots in the mulch, your face
Courting the camera's heart. The shutter clicks
And off you go to sniff all crones and grace
All trees with piss before a smaller box

Arrives to collect the last of the dust to fall.
Some old limbs creaked that night. I heard their call.

Leslie Porreca, *Pete*, photograph

Making a River

make it part cat slipping through a field
of winter wheat and part woman
a hissing dance through pocket water
give it the shape of trout or mink
and cliffs and a path
let it lay claim to valleys and mountains
dragging down trees sometimes cottages
put a chalky moon in it and old bones
and give it memory of where it's been
call it Loyalsok or Little Juniata
make it lonely on certain evenings
and let it end the way a season ends
into something larger than itself

From the collection of the Managing Editor, photograph

I wanted to sit

in the old parlor with its three sofas
and two windows

with dawn coming on and fog
in the hollows above the river

and the mountain yellow and red
I wanted to stay for an hour

or maybe a day
watching for the black bear

to waddle toward suet nailed to the oak
I wanted to touch

the rattlesnake skin on one wall
the Latin book on the shelf

and to hear voices and floor creak
and leave with some old word

on my tongue

Crime Scene

Sweeping up as the blonde came by
She caught my eye
"Nobody home, gone to the woods"
There she stood.
I could have said, "Go away!"
"Come again some other day."
Not "Come in!" as she did —
broke the chair, ate the porridge,
unmade the beds —
frightened little bear to pieces
when he found her in his bed.

Whippoorwill

Our Mama taught us to be still
and listen to the whippoorwill,
to look for violets in the grass,
to watch the ladies' hats at Mass,
to cross the Canal and breathe the salt air,
see a girl in the moon with a rose in her hair.

Neighbor Who Moved Away

Whirring hummingbird flits
from larkspur to fuchsia
gathers morning nectar
and whirls into orbit.

Seven months since you left
and you may draw sweet peas
with a silent hummer
unhurried in his day.

I do not picture where
you live and cannot send
a slip of rosemary.
Do you have a garden?

But life moves on
even though no Chinese artist
painted on silk scroll
the garden of farewell.

Sex at Seventy

*after Issa**

This morning we're having a rollicking good time in
bed, doing things we haven't done in years. My
goodness! You'd think we'd want to keep this hidden
from public view, to keep what happens in the house
in the house; we'd want to be discreet. But no,
here we are unveiling lips and tongue and teeth
until nothing that we could possibly do is left
to anyone's imagination. Come on in
and join us. You there! Yes, you! Who says the
old aren't sexual beings, too? Is your mouth
filled with laughter? We're laughing, too, but
it's a beatific laughter, laughter so feel-good
it becomes us. We *are* the laughter, and, with luck,
will be the laughter, no matter what abounds.

---

*The author calls the poems on these pages "golden shovel haiku sonnets"
and notes that "the last words of each line of each poem, read vertically
top to bottom, form a haiku by Japanese poets Basho, Issa, Buson, or
Onitsura."

Durian Fruit

after Basho

It tastes like turpentine and old gym socks! they say. It
tastes more like fungi, I think, puréed parsnips, though skunk is
not so far off. A custardy duff, it's not unlike oysters.
It looks like a naked mole rat! they complain. I'm not
in complete disagreement: "You can eat them dried,"
I try, "but it's better to savor the glutinous smoothness." *Seaweed
paste!* they say. It's true. Not to mention the fecal smell that
gets them outlawed in public places. And yet: "Eat one
bite!" I say. "You'll want another. The 'King of Fruits' should
be distinctive!" Still, no matter how hard I try to sell
my granddaughters on my whimsies and nostalgias, when
one can choose rose apple or the jackfruit of youth, one
is hard put to want leaf mold, no matter how sweet it is.
They'll turn up their nose at the rank musty smell of the old.

After Basho

after Basho

There are over 100 translations of Basho's frog. The
literal version, phonetically, reads thus: *Fu-ru* (old)
i-ke (pond) *ya ka-wa-zu* (frog) — or, old pond
frog — *to-bi-ko-mu* (jumping into) *mi-zu* (water) — or, a
jumping into water — *no o-to* (sound). The frog
doesn't care if he's lost in translation. He jumps
anyway, and his meaning jumps with him. In
English, that frog water sound might be *kerplunk!*
I have my own small pond in the country. Now
and then, as I walk around it, a frog jumps in. The
sound it now makes, after Basho, is always the sound
of Basho's frog. The sound of the water is the sound of
his famous haiku, or "play verse," to translate the
term literally. An old pond. Basho jumps into the water.

The Man in the Rain

after Buson

Sometimes things just slip out of existence: the
set of keys, the wallet, the cherished photo, all ferry
themselves off to who knows where? A thing departs
of its own accord, leaving you as bereft as
if it had intentionally abandoned you, the
vanishing enough to bring you down. The last
thing you want to be is to be left behind, the tardy
man whose friends and family have departed, the man
alone on the dock of his life, the man who stands
at a loss, unable quite to figure out what in
God's name has become of them. Which is the
most lost? That which is gone? Or that which first
noticed it missing? Summer, which sails off? Or winter,
which remains? The dear departed? Or the man in the rain?

The Rapture

after Basho

Did the pilot really say, "I'll see you in
a future life"? We're flying over the
South China Sea, I think. Outside, the bitter
cold would kill us, or at least give us a "radish"
as my four-year-old granddaughter called the rash that
covered her bottom with what was probably bug bites
from a night spent at Bible camp. We're flying into
a thunderstorm. The lightning looks to me
like the apocalypse; the rapture, perhaps, I
am thinking how we mistake things. How the feel
of foreignness is unnerving, or at least funny. The
"future life"? A "radish"? Sometimes icy cold
can be perceived as hot. Sometimes autumn
seems like spring. The voice of God, the wind.

My Husband's Last Garden

1.
Little bud, little red bud
I summon you to deliver him.
Dash his grim march.
Cave the rattling terror.
Ration despair in dainty teaspoons
all the better to swallow, my dear.

Stamen and pistil,
I summon your rapture
Each filament — slender, yellow-tipped
the petals' crimson blaze.

2.
Ophelia named them as she wove
death prettily. Virginia Woolf
felt branches flick,
waded deeper, rocks
in her pockets.

3.
Stage one: victim assumes a near-
vertical position in water, arms flailing
legs still.

Stage two: water in mouth, epiglottis closed
as victim holds breath.

4.
Dazed by the gritty touch of another day.
There is a willow grows aslant the brook
lovely lure of water. You, too, swallowed,
saltwater gushing down throat,
flowing through nostrils, sealing
ears. Gracesong filling your lungs.

5.
Gardens know a thing or two
about dying.

Prickle of frost, days
shortened to gray blink.
Everywhere the barren.

6.
Stage three: respiratory arrest,
rate of sinking dependent on body weight, muscle
mass, amount of air trapped in lungs.

Hypoxic convulsion stage, body
rigid, blue. Mouth and nose foaming.

Final stage: cardiac arrest.

If he is found after a week:
skin peeled to dermis, sticky redbrown
of putrative heolysis

gaseous swelling of face and eyeballs,
tongue protruding, ballooned to ghastly plug.

7.
Lover of long-ago words
dissected in college
The Wasteland a fixture
on your bedstand
bones and rocks
drowned Phoenician sailor
no rain blooming corpse.
Fire speaks burning burning.
Said Madame Sosostris,
Fear death by water.

8.
Body teetering on rail
how long

before you jumped you left the house

in early morning
azaleas and camellias sleeping

but what about the hush
in windless trees

you left behind
you left the house

in early morning light still dreaming

From the collection of the Editor, photograph

Late Bloomers

End of August, up
the naked ladies send
their hard-earned blush,
lily faces boldly pink,
rows of them beyond
the bank of ivy,
startling against
the paling sky.
Not from nowhere —
don't be fooled —
months, years
they've brooded
under mulch, cuttings.
One day their stems
appear barely noticed
until foliage drops away

like ours, sisters underneath
with thinning hair.
We've heard
the whirr of diagnostic
rays, breasts jammed
between glass plates,
held our breath in wait.
Today, as fall
comes crawling,
we rise to the occasion
in a rush of pink
after the run, rows of us
shoulder-pressed and
several deep, brilliant
in this hour,
more to come.

My Everything

Since I no longer have a husband,
everything else has become mine: always
family and friends, my house, now
my beach, moon, hummingbird, every gopher
who dines on every last root, mine —

especially my field —
the one I've lived behind for forty years,
the one that loves me so much, every day
it combs its hair a different way,
changes shirts to match my mood.

A gate separates us. But I have
the key to enter, roam over its strong breast
whenever I choose. Some mornings
my field sends a red-tail hawk flashing
the sky, a pack of coyotes, noses pressed
against the chain-link fence.

"You're beautiful," I sing, charmed
with their wildness, empty-handed.
They skip off sideways at my advance,
return for more.

Last night against the dark sky,
I noticed my oak holding hands with my elm.
At the center of its heart, a light pulsed
from nowhere through thinning leaves.

Just as you left me, field spoke
and scooped me up, my everything.

Love Game

In a movie, teens use "Tic-Tac-Toe"
to teach a defense computer the nonsense
of nuclear conflict. Unable to line up
three of a kind, the machine decides
the way to win is not to play.

Children in ancient Rome scrawled
on walls and learned the same lesson
as kids today, who go back to making
their way down the row of monkey bars
risking a fall, one arm at a time;

back to seesaws, where their place
in the world moves always up and down.
Back to the love game, "Hide and Seek,"
where at the end they find someone
and are themselves, joyfully, found.

Eleanor Leonne Bennett, photograph

Eden Deferred

The last time you entered this greenhouse,
says the head gardener, the jasmine withered beneath
your touch. *Tu mal de ojo — your evil eye — jinxed*
my kalanchoes, melted the wax vine off its stem,
thwarted my violets. Not even the cacti survived.

Impossible! I reply. I may be foreign to your ways,
but I can coax my plants into blooming under
midnight moons, snip deadheads, sink toes deep
into alien soil, sing to my garden in Spanish.

Waving my urgency in his face, I beg for access.
Nothing personal, señorita. Arms crossed, he turns,
enters his steamy Eden, where buried beneath
an alphabet of blooms — acacia, broom, calendula,
daisy, edelweiss . . .words germinate.

Holding on

is hard for me

as if my hands
do not receive the relay
that tells them how tightly

to grasp onto things: chalk,
for instance, pencils, glasses,
grapes, cheese, car keys,

a job I loved much better
after I left it, a cell biologist
I knew too well, the cottage

on the Cape, the old blue
raincoat, the Keds with holes
in all the right places

and soft broken laces.

Skate

When no one else was skating,
I went down to the golf course pond,
laced up my skates, pushed off and
crossed the ice
knock-kneed, my ankles at right angles.

Neptune-blue, the evening air.
All my friends and all of theirs
at supper.

As it grew night, all I could see—
a round of white on any side of me.
Defeated once again,
a sea-monster in quest of grace
on land, or half-land half-lake.
Instead I headed home

where my potted tangerine
had spit me out five tiny blooms,
stunk the whole house into a hair salon

while just outside my window,
Io popped volcanoes,
one by one.
Good job, well done, by a superior moon.

Promenade

Accompanied by pelicans,
two old slatterns dressed in bells
by the sweets stalls promenaded
sucking licorice and chocolate.

Nickels jingled in their pockets,
just enough for caramels.
Along came sandpipers and gulls.
What a pretty fare-thee-well,

you and me, dear, on the boardwalk,
candy, birds and bells.

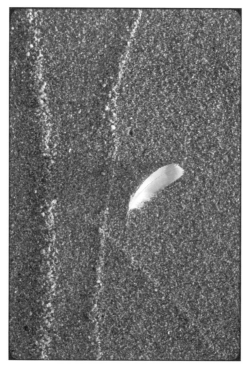

Steve Lautermilch, photograph

Annie in Motion

Annie circles the gym
as if she's sailing on a windblown lake,
as if to run is effortless, a whim.
Annie circles the gym.
To run is happiness—to skim
the waves and bend them to her wake.
Annie circles the gym
as if she's sailing on a windblown lake.

When Annie swims, she flies—slim-
winged butterfly startling a sky-blue pool,
moving from an impetus of symmetry within.
When Annie swims, she flies, slim
arms loosing drops that catch the sun and trim
the air with circling jewels.
When Annie swims, she flies, slim-
winged butterfly startling a sky-blue pool.

The water owns her destination
but the air is her milieu
when Annie dives. It's all about elation.
The water owns her destination.
What happens on the way is her creation,
her discipline, the site of her *prie-Dieu*.
The water owns her destination
but the air is her milieu.

May it survive, her *joie de vivre*,
when she grows up—as children will.
Even in sadness, let her still dream, believe.
May it survive, her *joie de vivre*,
on days when she loses, days she may grieve
as she grows tall and calm and still.
May it survive, her *joie de vivre*,
when she grows up, as children will.

Mill Town

No poetry here, not in this shire,
no quiet, solitary hours, writing,
just peas and biscuits warming on the fire,
farmhands and sheepdogs coming and going.

No sweet trolling the page, word by word,
just draughts from the cup of forgetting,
and stories told of the workaday world,
and plates to be washed in the sink, waiting.

Just sleep abiding in the clearing
at the deep, dark center of the day,
children napping, a mother bearing
news, together with the smell of old hay.

Leslie Porreca, photograph

A Common Life

It's possible to be with someone who's gone.
—Linda Gregg

He didn't want her
when he was younger and now he does.
Claims his first affair, which made everything go wrong,
his fling with the flamenco dancer, was a big mistake.
The daughter of the hotelkeeper in Barcelona, the man
who counted them among his foreign friends. Early evening
she saw them through the rain-smeared window of the garden shed.
The girl in her red skirt straddled him on a chair.
What she remembers twenty years later is the skirt,
its flame and flare, how it looked as if their pale, naked
torsos rose from the skins of large flayed animals
she'd weep for in her dreams. The mistake lasted three nights,
the girl crying on the platform as they, husband and wife,
caught the train, the second-class carriage, bulb burnt out in the toilet,
shit splattering the toilet seat and floor, their lovemaking ten years
into their marriage so tender she knew she'd be alone by Paris.
Now she's counting cormorant crucifixions on the rocks
in English Bay. Practicing her Spanish, she says out loud
uno, dos, tres, quatro. Ocho is the number she likes best,
its noisy *ch* in the centre, its perfect rhyme.
There were others—she'd heard it from their friends—
more as he got famous, the reps paid to pick him up,
a whirl of signings, single malts and undone buttons,
dirty towels on bathroom floors. It was easy to fall
for his face, the same photo he'd used for years,
clipped white beard and hair, head bent,
eyelids half closed. His sensitivity and sorrow
beautifully posed. Now he's back. Yesterday he left
The Divine Comedy on her doorstep. Signed, as if he'd written it.
Later in the evening he phoned. Said every lover in his poems
was her, every loss, every happiness accounted for was her.
This morning, on her way home with groceries, she saw him
sitting in a car outside the house. She turned and walked back
the way she came, pushing into wind as if she pushed a cart

the two blocks to the ocean. If they'd stayed together,
they'd be grandparents now, they'd be sitting in the sun
somewhere. If they were lucky they'd be sweetly irked by one another.
They'd tell the stories of a common life. The truth is
she believes him, in some small place she knows he never left.
There were lovers after him, of course, three of them
long term, one a husband, all of them now dead.
She can't stop thinking of their withered seeds
inside her, dry and small as isotopes
shot into a prostate to make a tumor shrink.
Sometimes at night between the sheets she glows.
What she loves now is the cold coming in
off the ocean, there's no age to it, no countenance,
and the birds, three times three, *nueve,*
miming crosses as they dry their wings,
are not wounded, at least not that she can see.

Reghina Gunzurevscaia, *Metamorphosis*, watercolor, 8" x 10"

Richard Wilbur Got It Backwards

in "Love calls us to the things of this world"

Love doesn't call us to this welter of need.
No, we fall into life amazed,
and flounder to stay afloat in the rush of years,
buoyed by our instincts to build or believe.

If we're lucky, some fact or artifact of this world
hijacks us, thank God. A gust
may snuff from the gutter a sudden sign.
Or among 12 billion human hands,
one somehow sculpts with skin and bone
the shape of itself.
Or lurching in rhythms of hunger and sleep,
we're tumbled together like scraps of two hearts
that touch, waver, syncopate —and match beats.

It's the fractal beauty of leaf, root and tree
or the perilous accident of place
that hurls us flailing into love.
The world grabs us —our only chance.

What Took You So Long?

1

Nick said that the will granted Ida lifetime rights to the house and its surrounding eight acres. Nothing would be sold before she died unless she agreed to it. Ida asked him if he wanted a drink. To assuage her concerns Nick had mentioned that he was the sole heir—he was quite comfortable with his Aunt Winifred's wishes. "Beer or something stronger?" Ida said. A lit cigarette hung from her frown, and behind blue smoke her face was a grille of February frost. Nick wondered, had Ida always been sharp edges and abrupt angles or had age stolen some hint of softness? Most likely she was never pretty. He had seen pictures of her, but she was well into her forties when the photos were taken. Handsome was the most you could have said about Ida and that was being kind. Before her, there were photos of Millie, but Nick had never met Millie, nor Ida for that matter, until that day when he told her the details of his aunt's will, as if she hadn't already known them; and they sat beside the creek, beneath hemlocks; and she used gardening shears to cut open the plastic bag of powdered ash and chips of bone.

"Here, you do the rest," she said, and Ida handed him the open bag, then lit a cigarette.

"Isn't there something we should say?" Nick asked. "Maybe read a favorite poem or prayer?"

"I've already said goodbye," Ida muttered. "This isn't Freddie. No way she'd be sealed in a bag. How's that for a prayer?" Maybe it was the cigarette smoke that caused Ida's eyes to tear. Nick whispered Amen.

He thinks of that day and tastes the shock of Ida's Bloody Marys, more vodka and hot sauce than tomato juice, as he unfolds a letter signed by Jonathan Wheaton, Esq., Skaneateles, New York, and then reads Ida's enclosed obituary. They had exchanged empty words—he and Ida—as empty as her obituary, which says nothing of his Aunt Winifred, just as Winifred's obituary had said nothing of Ida.

The house is now Nick's to do with as he pleases. Only his. No kids to consider and, as of four months ago, no wife either. An amicable divorce, little fuss over money. She made more than he did anyway; Nick could keep his teacher's salary. No pets. She was allergic to dander, cats and dogs, or so she said. Plants? Who had time to water them? However, she had found time for affairs. He pretended not to notice, like he pretended not to notice the birth control pills she said she had stopped taking after he suggested children, only a suggestion—Nick wasn't one to make demands. Ultimately, his wife's indiscretion with a delivery boy, one of Nick's high school students, would be his final humiliation. When he asked her for a divorce, she simply smiled and said, "What took you so long?"

He folds Ida's empty obituary. Selling his aunt's house might be just the distraction he needs. He remembers little of the house except that like many tired, old farmhouses it was in a state of quaint decline and its furnishings were flea market, circa 1950. No heirlooms would be discovered amid the laminate and Naugahyde, but the surrounding trees are magnificent, and it's only four hours from the George Washington Bridge. He can use a change of scenery before starting his new teaching position.

❉ ❉ ❉

The crushed stone driveway announces Nick's arrival. A forest of conifers and deciduous trees gives way to threesomes and couples and solitary specimens framing the driveway and house. Did he inherit his love of trees from his aunt? Except for random facts, Nick knows little of his Aunt Winifred: she was his father's only sibling and ten years his father's senior, served as a WAC in World War II, graduated from Wells College, worked as a school social worker, hated the name Winifred, owned a house upstate and had a *friend*, Ida, whose very name caused Nick's mother to roll her eyes. He had been in Winifred's company at family gatherings—holidays, graduations, weddings, funerals, etc.—but Nick found her, like his paternal grandparents, to be aloof, or, as his mother said, cold.

Nick's father was from white, Protestant stock, dating back to Mayflower times, but his mother was second-generation Sicilian, and Nick grew up mostly among Sicilians and other Italians, a stark contrast to his father's family. Plus, there were bad feelings. Nick's paternal grandparents and aunt felt that his father was marrying down, in fact they didn't attend his parents' wedding, and Nick's mother was not one to forgive, ever, even after Nick was born and his grandparents spent their remaining years making amends, especially after his father died prematurely. "A curse," his mother said, "from your father's heartless parents."

Nick's mother had often complained to his father, "You know damn well that if Winifred had found a husband and given your parents grandchildren, we'd never hear from them." But there was no discussion about why Winifred hadn't found a husband, just rolling eyes and snide remarks. And Nick's grandparents, already tightlipped, were mute about Winifred. The only hint that Winifred was more than a list of random facts was the ring of photographs circling her bedroom mirror, her childhood bedroom in her parents' house, where she slept when she visited and where she moved back during her parents' declining years. "Who's that, Aunt Winifred?" "Ida," she answered. "And that, Aunt Winifred?" "Millie," she answered. And no matter how many times Nick asked her, she offered the same terse response. He learned not to ask questions.

From the front porch he looks out across Willowdale Road, where acres of hayed land slope away to hedgerows of willows and sugar maples and ash trees. He views glimmers of Otisco Lake through breaks in the hedgerows, and beyond the lake are more hills, mostly wooded, but with patches of farmland. Above the hills, blue-white clouds, like immense vaporous circus animals, lumber across the sky and draw giant shadows along the landscape.

Inside the house smells of shut windows and loneliness. Less faded patches of wood flooring and carpet and wallpaper speak of missing furniture. The lawyer assured Nick that Ida's nieces had removed only *their* aunt's belongings. Maybe a greatniece or greatnephew was furnishing a college apartment. Who else would want such junk? One room is empty, except for a photograph of his aunt—probably Ida's bedroom, or a study. Another bedroom, most likely Winifred's, has numerous framed photographs hanging on walls or perched on a dresser. As in her old bedroom in Nick's grandparents' house, pictures are taped around a mirror. He recognizes his grandparents and Ida and maybe Millie. But there are others, not familiar. Snapshots of Winifred's life: picnics and boating and fishing and cross-country skiing. On a desk is a studio portrait of Winifred and Ida resembling each other the way old couples do. There's also a small picture Winifred must have taken of Nick at his college graduation.

Nick unpacks his few things and, in the dresser, places shirts and underwear and socks atop his aunt's clothes, then hangs a pair of jeans and a rain jacket in the closet when he hears: "Hello! Anyone here? Hello!"

Nick closes the closet door and steps from Winifred's bedroom and down the steep creaking stairs back to the living room. The front door is ajar, and a man leans into the house while his feet remain planted on the porch.

"You Nick? Freddie's nephew?" The man asks.

"Yes," Nick answers. He remembers that Ida had called his aunt Freddie.

"I'm Merrill. Been keepin' an eye on this place since Ida went to the hospital. I figured you'd show up sooner or later."

Merrill's about the same age as Nick, fiftyish,, and though his tanned skin is lined around his smile and his hair thinning at the crown, Merrill reminds Nick of his students. Maybe it's Merrill's wiry build, or the way his t-shirt is half tucked into his grass-stained jeans, or the way he looks Nick right in the eyes as if he hasn't yet learned not to trust.

"I received a letter and the obituary from the lawyer," Nick says.

Merrill shakes his head, "Yeah, lung cancer. Ida smoked like a chimney. Lousy way to go. She stayed here almost to the end. She was a tough one. Mind if I come in? Holdin' this door open, I'm invitin' flies."

"No . . . I mean, sure, I don't mind. I just got here myself."

Merrill kicks off his shoes and lets the screen door slam behind him. The big toe of his right foot peeks through a hole in his sock and there's black under his fingernails. Nick wonders if Merrill works one of the local farms.

"Sorry I can't offer you a beer or something, but please sit down." Nick looks around the room. "Guess that's easier said than done. Not much to sit on."

"You sit there," Merrill says. He points to a well-worn recliner and raises his voice as he disappears through an open door: "I'll get a chair from the kitchen. Yeah, I saw one of Ida's nieces an' some kid load up a U-Haul. A couple of her nieces used to visit once in a while, more as Ida got sicker." Merrill walks back into the living room carrying a chrome kitchen chair with a gray and red vinyl back and seat. Much of the vinyl is cracked. "Guess they just about emptied the place."

The men sit facing each other. Nick's jeans and t-shirt speak of Manhattan, a stroll through Central Park and a beer at Tavern On The Green; Merrill's jeans and t-shirt speak of jeans and a t-shirt.

"You're lucky they left that." Merrill points to a painting—oil, sharp contrasts between dark and light, an arc of boughs, a bracken of ferns, rocks, and fallen trees interrupt the rush of water, splashes of light against dark browns and greens, a spring representation of the November creek where Nick and Ida had left Winifred's ashes.

Nick examines the painting. "I recognize that spot."

"Their favorite," Merrill says.

"Their?"

"Freddie an' Ida. They loved it. The creek runs along the west side of the land, borderin' what used to be the Sharps' place. In summer Freddie an' Ida sat there before dinner an' had their drinks. Cocktails, they called them. We had plenty of picnics by that creek. Freddie an' Ida an' the Sharps an' me an' Victor, an' sometimes musician friends come visit for most of the summer. I don't know how they managed in this little house, but they did. Those were good times. Once, one of your aunt's dogs . . . you know she always had those corgis, looked like God forgot to give them legs . . . well it came nose to nose with a tiny fawn that was all curled up in the tall weeds. There they were, just starin' at each other tryin' to figure things out while we was drinkin' our cocktails. Freddie grabbed the dog's collar an' the fawn stood up on its skinny legs an' wobbled up into the woods callin' its mama. Freddie loved nature. She knew the name of every kind of tree an' wildflower. Like one of those guidebooks."

"Sounds like you knew my aunt well."

"'Bout as well as a person could know another. Real nice lady. Funny. Ida wasn't so funny, but still nice. Anyways, it's a good thing Ida's niece left that painting. Victor's stuff always sold pretty good but got pricier after he died. I'd say you could get a couple of thousand bucks for that one. Funny how what folks do is better appreciated after they're gone. Anyways, I just stopped by to introduce myself. You know, in case you need somethin'. You're probably gonna sell, but you should do a little paintin' or fixin' first, so you get a better price. The house ain't much, but the land's pretty. I helped plant a lot of the trees." Merrill stands and extends his right hand. "Real nice meetin' you. You need anythin', I'm pretty good at fixin' things. I live right down the road. The old Victorian at the four corners, across from the schoolhouse. Just turn right, out of your driveway. Less than a mile."

Victorian, Nick thinks. *Guess I had that wrong.*

           ✿   ✿   ✿

At some point during his teen years, Nick had assumed that his aunt was a lesbian, but he didn't give it much thought. His father's family was always reclusive, Winifred just a little more so, but as he sits on the front porch listening to the trill of tree frogs and the drum of a bullfrog, he imagines his aunt's life here with Ida, a full life that could never have flourished under rolling eyes and snide remarks. He wonders if Winifred and Ida were in fact lovers or if the weight of oppressive times had confined them to their separate bedrooms. Regardless, they were a couple and from the little Merrill said it appears as if they were happy—happier than Nick had been in his marriage.

Above dark undulating hills the sky is awash in pink and orange. Nick picks at macaroni and cheese, a box mix he found in the cupboard. What might it be like to live here? Merrill mentioned that across from his house is a school, but Nick can't imagine a school located in such a remote area, though he also can't imagine Merrill living in a Victorian house. Soon Nick would begin teaching at a new school; why not make a big change? Like his aunt, he could build a life away from rolling eyes and snide remarks. It's not too late. He leans against the porch railing taking in the silhouettes of trees and of bats feasting on insects. Not Manhattan, but is that so bad?

Later, through his open bedroom window, an owl's mantra lulls him. Wasn't Merrill too young and, considering Winifred's attitude, too illiterate to have been her friend, and what was the artist's name? Victor. Nick's glad that Ida's niece left the painting and glad that Merrill visited. Friendly enough guy. It's been years since Nick's felt glad about anything. He draws a frayed quilt up over his shoulder.

           ✿   ✿   ✿

Morning fog obscures Otisco Lake, but by the time Nick showers and shaves and slips on his jeans and a fresh t-shirt, then drives his car left onto Willowdale, the fog has lifted or burned off or whatever fog does when it dissipates. He retraces yesterday's drive past farmhouses, some in the same disrepair as his aunt's or worse, some restored. He also passes trailers and an eclectic mix of new homes, modest doublewides and large contemporaries with expansive windows. A dairy farm to Nick's right on the downhill side of the road appears abandoned except for cows grazing in a pasture or peeking out of a dilapidated barn or standing alongside the road as if they're waiting for a bus. The farmhouse is overgrown with sumac and grapevine and the skeletal barns lean precariously. Feral cats vanish like wizards into clumps of chicory and Queen Anne's lace.

The GPS advises Nick to turn left, up a road he hasn't traveled, where rows of corn soak up the morning sun. A flock of wild turkeys awkwardly take flight. Nick meanders upwards through the cornfields, until he reaches Route 41, where he turns right onto the crest of the hill between Otisco and Skaneateles Lakes, towards the village of Skaneateles. To his left is a pull-off overlooking the expanse of Skaneateles Lake, more elegant than Otisco, and it glitters under the morning sun as if boasting of its splendor. It's a ten-minute drive to the village where stately homes lounge on expansive lawns accessorized with hydrangea and hibiscus and framed with ornate wrought iron. Gradually these mini-estates morph into commercial buildings—on the lakeside is a stretch of attached two-story brick buildings, with first-floor shops and second-floor condos.

After parking his car and buying a coffee and scone in one of the village shops, Nick finds a bench in the lakeside park where the view of sailboats and Gatsbian estates is stunning, and he savors the taste and texture of his coffee-splashed scone. Folks stroll the promenade along the lake, but Nick watches an elderly couple, returning arm in arm from their walk on the pier. Had Winifred and Ida enjoyed this lakeside paradise, exchanging greetings with the locals, nodding at tourists? He can't imagine Merrill in this village, but then Merrill is an enigma, with his grimy fingernails and his holey socks and his homey vernacular, but with stories of sipping cocktails, and again Nick wonders about the artist Victor? Merrill had mentioned " . . . me and Victor." Did he mean as a couple?

Nick shrugs and tosses the last few crumbs of his scone to some tenacious ducks.

Across the street is a real estate office, and Nick's impressed by the hefty prices of the listings in the window, not just lakeside mansions, but also smaller, more modest homes throughout the village. From a conversation with the Realtor, he learns that Skaneateles prices are an anomaly and that homes in the Otisco Lake area sell for less. She tells him that buyers from New York City and Long Island are amazed by the bargains they find here in Central New York. "Of course that's good news for the buyer, not the seller," she chuckles. She hands Nick her card, "But I'm sure that I could get you a good price. You said the house has a view of the lake? Otisco is one of the Finger Lakes' best kept secrets. Just lovely." He pockets the agent's card, thanks her, asks where's the closest supermarket, then makes his way back to his car. After grocery shopping he tours the village side streets, admiring the modest but well kept homes with the hefty price tags. He passes Skaneateles High School and remembers that before last year he had loved teaching.

✺ ✺ ✺

To the right of Nick's house the roadsides are more heavily wooded. A mangy white dog bounds up to Nick, tail wagging. "Hey, boy!" Nick bends to pet the dog, then they walk together as if they are long-time buddies. Nick spots a school under a canopy of sugar maples, an old one-room schoolhouse with a belfry and a fresh coat of white paint. A sign stands close to the road—Side-Hill School, but Nick can't read the smaller print.

Beyond the trees, to Nick's right, is a Victorian house, high-gabled and draped in gingerbread. Like the schoolhouse it's freshly painted, but with multiple colors; resplendent gardens border the foundation, and the lawn looks more like carpet than grass. This can't be Merrill's house. The white dog barks as if announcing Nick, and Merrill appears from out of a small barn, which is nearly as impeccable as the house.

"Hey, Hobo, you brought a visitor." Merrill holds a wrench. He runs his right forearm across his face, smearing grease or soil on his left cheek, and smiles. "Just let me clean up," Merrill says, then disappears back into the barn.

Nick walks up to the house. No caked or chipped paint, every detail is perfect, as if it were built yesterday.

"You like these kinds of houses?" Merrill startles Nick. His hair is wet and freshly combed, and he smells of soap.

"There's a place, a short ferry ride from Sag Harbor . . . Long Island," Nick says. "We used to vacation there when we were first . . . I mean I used to go there years ago. There were a lot of houses like this, some not much bigger than a doll's house."

"This one's Queen Anne," Merrill folds his calloused hands behind his back and nods his scruffy chin as if lecturing, "but all that fancy stuff is called Eastlake after Charles Eastlake."

Nick stares at him incredulously. Who is this man? Again, Merrill reminds Nick of his students, attempting to impress the teacher, but unguarded, innocent. Though innocent might not be the right word for high school boys, considering that a twelfth-grader in Nick's American Literature class copulated with Nick's wife, then boasted of his conquest to every student in the small private high school.

"It was built by a Methodist minister, hoping to build more an' turn his land into some kind of religious camp. Not sure why it didn't work out, but there's all kinds of stories. Mostly idle gossip. You know how small-minded folks can be." Merrill punctuates his commentary with a nod and a broad smile. "Wanna go inside?"

Before Nick has a chance to answer, Merrill's on the porch, removing his shoes and holding the screen door open for Nick. Nick follows him, then bends to remove his own shoes. "No need. Mine's always dirty, but you look like you just stepped out of a magazine." Nick blushes, something he has no recollection of ever doing.

The interior accents are even more pristine than the exterior gingerbread—high-gloss hardwood floors and wainscoting, coving arches at the juncture of walls and ceilings, an entry hall staircase with ornate, fluted newel posts and balusters. The two parlors and dining room are replete with European antiques, intricately carved and heavily lacquered; upholstery is plush and of warm subdued golds and greens and burgundies, as are the drapes that hang from heavy rods trimmed with gilded finials. On the walls are tapestries and oils, similar to the lone painting in Nick's sparse living room. "Yes, Victor did those," Merrill says as Nick observes the paintings.

"This place is amazing," Nick doesn't add — Are you sure that you live here?

"An' a bear to clean, just ask Violet," Merrill says.

"Violet?"

"Yeah, she's the one who keeps this place so spotless. I take care of the outside an' Violet takes care of the inside. Used to be my granma who done the cleaning an' most of the cooking." Merrill lifts a silver-framed photograph from a fringed scarf covering a baby grand piano and hands it to Nick. "That's Granma an' me."

A sepia Merrill, about twelve years old, folds himself into the pleats of an old woman's apron. They stand next to lilacs in full bloom. As Nick returns the photo to the piano, he eyes other photos of Merrill at various ages and one of Merrill with an older man. The man is tall and slender and formal in his dress and posture.

"That's me an' Victor," Merrill says. "He'd fasten the camera to a tripod, have us pose, then he'd run back an' set something on the camera, then run back next to me an' the camera would shoot the picture. I was never much of a photographer. Victor always took the pictures. Guess it was the artist in him. I'll show you upstairs, then we'll get somethin' to drink."

The second-floor furnishings are as opulent as the first floor's. Beyond the master bedroom is what Merrill calls a tea porch. There is also a smaller bedroom, and as they pass a closed door, Merrill mentions that it's to Victor's studio.

The kitchen is bright and more functional than decorative. An old farmer drives a honey wagon down Willowdale Road, and a whiff of aged manure drifts through the screen door and open kitchen windows. Hobo sniffs at the air as Merrill points to a room off the kitchen. "That's my room." There are books stacked on a nightstand, which surprises Nick.

"Lemonade?" Merrill asks.

They sit at a small kitchen table and Nick speaks of his conversation with the Skaneateles realtor.

Merrill chuckles, "Yeah, some maps of the Finger Lakes don't even show Otisco . . . like it's a bastard kid. May be one of the runts, but if you ask me it's the prettiest, especially the southwest part, right below us. Tomorrow we'll drive down to the lake in the gator."

"I'd like that," Nick says, though he has no idea what a gator is.

The worst part of Nick's wife having had an affair with his student was how people changed after it: students averted their eyes and giggled, and faculty avoided conversations that went beyond discussing the weather. Nick's mother summed it up perfectly: "Well, it's late, but finally you're rid of that bitch." Merrill doesn't know about any of this, instead he rambles on about how his family has lived in this area forever, and his great-grandfather, then his grandfather owned a boat livery on the east side of Otisco, until his grandfather drowned when he got tangled up in his fishing line, and after the family lost the livery his grandma went to work for Victor. And all the while Merrill talks, he looks right at Nick and there's no pity in Merrill's eyes, and Nick can't help but enjoy the refreshing company of this unassuming man.

After a deep breath and a swallow of lemonade, Merrill asks, "So when do you think you'll sell?"

"I don't know. Maybe I won't sell. Maybe they can use an English teacher in Skaneateles."

Merrill laughs. "Now wouldn't that be something."

"I'm just thinking aloud."

"Well you keep thinkin' that way. With Ida gone, seems like all folks do is leave here."

"Do you miss her?" Nick's surprised by his own words. He's not one to question. "Sorry, I didn't mean to pry."

"That's okay. I miss all of them. Guess that's the problem with having friends that are old. They up an' die on you, or they move to Florida. That's what the Sharps did . . . the couple that lived on the other side of the creek from Freddie an' Ida. It's like I'm also old, but I'm not near dyin' and I don't think I'd like Florida." Merrill chuckles.

Nick doesn't think of Merrill as old. If anything, he seems to Nick like one of Peter Pan's lost boys, and earlier, when Nick viewed the photograph of a young Merrill with the tall and slender and much older Victor, he got a queasy feeling, but then Nick is a pro at dismissing feelings, queasy or otherwise.

Early the next day while the sun still shines on the west side of Otisco Lake, before it disappears behind the heavily treed shoreline, they drive the gator, which resembles a heavy-duty golf cart, down the steep, rutted, winding road past ravines and abrupt drop-offs, which Merrill says are waterfalls in the spring, but now they're barely trickles. After Merrill parks the gator, they traverse the many steps down past a wall of ferns and myrtle and bare tree roots, like corroding anchors that might give way to a sylvan landslide. They pass the remnants of a stone fireplace and chimney; beyond this is a shed, then along the shale shoreline are a rowboat with a small outboard motor and two kayaks. "Been a dry summer," Merrill says, "Lake hasn't been this low since '96."

The lake mirrors the blue sky and the shadows of gulls and a great blue heron. Merrill opens the shed door and removes two lifejackets and paddles. He slips one of the jackets over his t-shirt with the image of a folksy trio and the words *Happiness is an Otisco Firehouse Pancake*, then hands Nick the other jacket and a pair of water shoes. "Zebra mussels. You'll cut up your feet."

"Those were Freddie an' Ida's." Merrill points to the two wooden kayaks leaning into each other. "Ida gave them to me after Freddie died, but I was just watchin' them. Kind of like I was watchin' the house. They're yours now. Do you like kayaking?"

"Never tried it," Nick says.

"Well, it's a good day to learn."

After a brief lesson on getting in and paddling, Nick's kayak glides easily, not far behind Merrill's. They hug the west shore of the lake, craggy and dense with hemlock and hornbeam, and beech and basswood, and ash and aspen, whose leaves flutter like the wings of a thousand silver butterflies. A regal sycamore dwarfs the other trees.

"Another plus for Otisco over Skaneateles," Merrill shouts.

"What's that?"

"Weekdays there's not much traffic on the lake. Come fall, it's even quieter."

Nick scans the lake. Merrill is right; there are more gulls and ducks than people. A largemouth bass breaks the water's surface.

Merrill waits for Nick to catch up. "On Skaneateles, all those folks with the fancy houses have to show off their fancy boats. It's like a damn pissin' contest. Sometimes Freddie an' Ida would drive their kayaks over the hill to Skaneateles, an' after they come back from fighting the wakes of those big, fancy power boats, Ida would complain about wastin' the day, an' Freddie would say somethin about the grass being greener. They liked bickerin'. Seemed like they just liked talkin' to each other." Nick finds it difficult to imagine his aunt being a talker, considering how quiet it was in his grandparents' house, even when his aunt was there.

"Unfortunately, I didn't know my aunt very well," Nick says.

Both men stop paddling; Merrill holds onto the rim of Nick's kayak; they drift into a bog of milfoil. Nick looks into the weeds and thinks of the books on Merrill's nightstand and asks a question that's not really about his aunt: "How long did you know Freddie?" This is the first time he calls his aunt Freddie and the first time he observes Merrill's eyes look inward.

"When Granma's cancer got bad we moved in with Victor, he was already good friends with Freddie an' Ida. I was about twelve. They helped me an' Victor take care of Granma, especially the personal stuff."

"I'm sorry," Nick says.

"'Bout what? Old folks die. It's only natural."

2

Before the school year begins, Nick resigns from his position at the new charter school in Manhattan and sublets his studio apartment. Skaneateles and other surrounding high schools are not hiring; his best offer is a tentative yes as a long-term sub to replace a teacher going on maternity leave in Homer, about twenty miles south, but the teacher's baby is not due until January. Violet, Merrill's housekeeper and, as it turns out, his cousin, had suggested that Nick apply at Homer High school, her daughter being the pregnant English teacher.

September is exceptionally warm and dry, and Merrill and Nick spend their days scraping and painting the outside of Nick's house. Victor may have been a master with oils on canvas, but Merrill is a master with latex on clapboards, and he's just as skilled at carpentry. The men share an easy rapport, and, without asking, Nick learns more about Freddie and Ida: stories about Freddie's job as a school social worker while Ida taught music at a small college, and they vacationed in the Adirondacks and on Cape Cod, and they had many friends and loved to entertain. Again, Merrill speaks of musician friends, some staying all summer. He speaks of summer nights filled with music and laughter and fireflies and of course cocktails, and Nick misses this aunt that he never really knew. Merrill doesn't say any more about his grandmother being sick or about when they moved in with Victor, and Nick doesn't ask, not that he doesn't have questions. Like why had Merrill come to live with his grandmother? Or why had he stayed with Victor after his grandmother died? And who was this Victor anyway? Nick left these questions in the bog of milfoil.

By the time evenings turn too cool for paint to set, Nick and Merrill have already begun working inside, and the refurbished farmhouse, cottage red with forest green trim, complements the changing leaves.

Now it's too beautiful a day to be inside and Merrill suggests a drive to the apple orchards. He'll show Nick where he's worked on and off since he was a kid, pruning trees and harvesting apples and pressing cider. Merrill has pieced together odd jobs his whole life. "When you're ready, give a call," Merrill says. "We'll go in my pickup."

Instead of calling, Nick walks to Merrill's house. The truck is in the driveway, but there's no sign of Merrill or of Hobo. During the past month and a half Nick's visited Merrill enough times to feel comfortable entering the house unannounced. He opens the kitchen door and calls Merrill's name, but there's no answer. He passes an empty coffee cup on the kitchen table and calls into the living room, then stands at the foot of the staircase to the second floor and calls again.

Nick barely hears Merrill's response: "In the attic. Come on up." Nick climbs to the second floor. "Which way?" he shouts at the ceiling. "Through the closet in the master bedroom," Merrill answers.

The first door Nick opens is to the bathroom, the second is to a room he doesn't recognize—Victor's studio. And Nick remembers his first time in the house and that he thought it was curious that this was the only room they didn't enter. The drapes are drawn, but despite the darkness, Nick observes outlines of large canvases, probably on easels, and more canvases propped against walls. The canvases on easels are covered with fabric, maybe tapestries. Soon his eyes would adjust to the dark.

"Did you find the stairs?" Nick hears Merrill's voice as if it comes from beneath a tapestry. He leaves the studio and closes the door behind him. A closet door in the master bedroom is ajar, and Nick enters, then climbs the stairs up to the attic.

"There you are," Merrill says. "I thought you got lost." With the steep pitch of the roof there's limited space for an adult to stand. A naked light bulb barely illuminates Merrill's back. He's hunched over in a corner, holding a flashlight. "From outside, I noticed a few holes in the eaves. Carpenter bees. With the heavy frosts, they're gone now. Just checkin' under this insulation to see if they drilled their way into the attic."

Nick hears the words *bees* and *insulation*, but his thoughts are in Victor's studio, and they linger there in the dark while he and Merrill drive to the orchards and pick apples and buy cider, and several times Merrill asks if something is bothering Nick and each time Nick answers no. After all, why should Nick care so much about those veiled canvases or Victor or for that matter Merrill? For someone who has long made a practice of not asking questions, now all Nick has are questions.

Before they leave the orchard, one of the owners complains to Merrill about being short-staffed; Merrill agrees to work for a few days and asks Nick to join him. "We can use a break from painting."

Come Monday, Nick feigns feeling ill. He knew that Merrill's house would be unlocked, but he didn't expect Victor's studio to be locked. He searches the kitchen and Merrill's bedroom for a key. Aside from books stacked on the nightstand, there's also a wall of bookshelves, and among how-to books are works of fiction, maybe Victor's, including classics by Wilde and Forster and Mann. A newspaper article spills out from a copy of *Death In Venice*.

Local Artist Dies In Fire
Victor Carpenter succumbs to smoke inhalation. Upon seeing smoke, boaters came ashore to find Carpenter face-down outside his burning camp. By the time fireboats arrived, the Otisco Lake camp was engulfed. Arson is suspected . . .

Nick sits at the edge of Merrill's bed and skims the article. At the time of the fire, Merrill, referred to as Carpenter's handyman, was repairing a barn on Willowdale Road. Nick sighs, returns the article to the book, slides open the drawer to the nightstand and discovers a key ring with a single key.

After he opens the drapes, light pours onto dust-covered tubes of dry paint and brushes and palettes and canvases leaning against walls and onto tapestries covering four canvases propped on easels. Through the dust he glimpses unfinished paintings of scenery and cursory portraits and sketches of nudes. He removes

one tapestry and another and another. Three paintings of the
young Merrill, nude and in classic poses: Pan, the God of the wild
with the hindquarters, legs, and horns of a goat; Ganymede being
abducted by Zeus in the form of an eagle; Narcissus mesmerized
by his own reflection. Nick recalls a trip to his maternal grandparents' hometown of Taormina, Sicily, where photographs by Baron
Wilhelm von Gloeden were on exhibit. Von Gloeden's most famous
pictures were of nude Sicilian boys — peasant youth with dirty
fingernails and dirty feet — in classic poses before the backdrop
of ancient ruins and Sicily's unforgiving landscape. Nick remembers his mother rolling her eyes the way she did when speaking
of Winifred. And he thinks of the first day he met Merrill and of
Merrill's dirty fingernails and his toe peeking through a hole in
his sock, but Merrill is a man. Not always. Not when he posed for
the paintings. *Arson suspected.* That's what the article said. Nick's
mind spins with thoughts of Merrill being the victim of the pedo-
phile Victor and Merrill taking his revenge. But hadn't Nick's high
school student bragged of fucking Nick's wife? Maybe Merrill at
eighteen, or twenty or twenty-five, was the seducer, for attention or
money or as a joke. Not Merrill. And Nick is weary of rolling eyes
and smirks and secrets and regrets the years he wasted in an empty
marriage.

One last canvas remains covered. But while Nick removes
the tapestry, he already knows why he cares so much about the
other paintings and why he is concerned about their implications.
He knows why he gave up his job and sublet his apartment and
moved into a house that was all but falling down. And when Nick
views the painting of the adult Merrill wearing a t-shirt and jeans
and sneakers and staring back at him, Nick knows the answer to
the question he feared most. For the past month and a half he's
been happier than he's ever been. "What took you so long?" Isn't
that the question his wife had asked him? Nick hears the front
door close. He doesn't cover the paintings or draw the drapes, nor
does he lock the studio door. In the living room Violet untangles
the vacuum-cleaner cord. Nick startles her.

"I thought you boys were working at the orchards," she says.
Violet is at most ten years older than Nick, but to her all men are
boys.

Nick sits on the steps; he's at eye level with Violet. "May I
ask you a question, Violet?" Just planning to question feels liberat-

ing to Nick. He's been in Violet's company a half-dozen times and likes her no-nonsense ways but doesn't know if he can trust her. It doesn't matter. Later, he plans to ask Merrill the same question anyway.

"Sure," Violet says. She plugs in the vacuum.

"Did Victor hurt Merrill?"

Violet looks at the key ring and key dangling from Nick's finger, then looks Nick in the eyes. She reminds Nick of Merrill. "Honey, that boy was hurt long before he ever met Victor. If anything Victor saved him."

Nick tries to object, but Violet holds up her long fingers as if she were stopping traffic. "I don't know what you think you just seen, but when Merrill come to live with our grandma he had stopped talking. Who knows which one of his mama's no-good boyfriends had stolen his voice or what else they took from him." Violet purses her lips as if she's about to spit. "When Grandma got sick Victor took them both in. No one else would have done that. My mama was working fulltime, and I was also working and pregnant with my first baby and my uncles lived far away and Merrill's mama wasn't worth the time of day. After Grandma died, you couldn't pry Merrill away from Victor. Why would you want to? Even after Victor was gone, he took care of that boy. He left enough money to keep Merrill in this house and to keep me cleaning it. Didn't your aunt ever tell you how Victor helped that boy? Now I got to start vacuuming or I'll never get my work done." Violet presses the toe of her shoe against the vacuum switch and Nick walks back upstairs. He draws the drapes and covers the paintings, then locks the door to Victor's studio. As he passes Violet on his way to Merrill's bedroom, she turns off the vacuum. "I take it you know where that key belongs," she says.

That evening, Nick sits on his porch. The air smells of wood smoke, and the moon is so bright Nick can barely see the stars. Hobo barks and Nick spots Merrill and Hobo approaching, and Nick wonders if their glow comes from the moon or from something within them. Merrill waves a half-gallon jug: "Fresh cider!" In his other hand there appears to be a fiddle. "Time for cocktails!" Merrill shouts. *Who is this man?* Nick thinks, and he can't help but smile.

My Parents' Health Declines

One afternoon, when she ordered her husband of almost six decades to stand up straight, he stayed in a slouch. They immediately put on coats and drove to his doctor, who diagnosed a stroke, and foretold imminent death.

Since her husband was the type to notice each morning whether he was alive or dead, and plan his day accordingly, the couple took their already-paid-for trip to Turkey (dismissing concerns of family who, as tactfully as they could, pointed out that, when it comes to dying, the familiar surroundings of home are preferable to somewhere so exotic). After Turkey, the couple traveled to Quebec, and then London. Before each departure, doctors pointed to statistical charts and, after each return, shrugged. By now he was almost blind.

They continued their subscription to the theater and their monthly book discussion group. And he continued to drive, with her beside him shouting, *Stop sign! Red light! Car!!!* until the out-of-town daughter insisted that only the mother could drive—although the mother's eyesight also was failing. Luckily, the father was still a good navigator—he knew the streets that well—so he could, at the right moments, call out, *Turn left at the third traffic light*, and, *Not this street, at the next, take a right.*

But for spotting other cars, the blindness handicapped him. One day on the highway: CRASH! car totaled. An ambulance rushed them to the nearest emergency room. By good fortune, other than a few bumps and cuts, they were fine. But now without wheels. A friend in their apartment building, who understood from personal experience such imprisonment, wrote down the phone number of a very nice man who sold cars to seniors and repaired them after accidents. From him, they bought their first used car, and more than once required his repair services.

Only after the wife appeared in court for hitting a firetruck did she stop driving—against her husband's protests. *She just nudged it*, he insisted. And, *The firetruck was only a small one!* Now, to get around, they were dependent on the kindness of their in-town daughter and those friends who still drove; and on the whims of the town's senior van, whose schedule required a degree of patience for which the wife had never been known.

To the consternation of family and friends, the husband elected to have eye surgery that required a year for recovery. And then expressed his determination to once again drive. Fortunately, the car had been sold back to the very nice man following the firetruck incident, saving the out-of-town daughter from having to say, *Absolutely not*.

They continued to do their own shopping. He held onto the cart for stability and slowly circumnavigated the store while she darted down each aisle they passed, grabbing groceries from the shelves and hurrying back to the cart before he reached the next aisle. They continued to go out to dinner at least once a week, though no longer to the fancier restaurants they had once frequented. The wife, who had always glared at any less-than-fastidious behavior, acted as though she didn't notice her husband's public hiccups and burps, or the food he spilled on his shirt and pants. Rather than interrupting him as she always had, she seemed to have discovered his good company, and asked frequently for his opinion or requested he tell a joke, listening attentively as he grasped for words. They paid for everything by credit card; she had him sign the bill.

Meanwhile, doctors argued over which of his many ailments was most likely to win the line on his death certificate. Dismissing such nonsense, the wife told her husband that, at a year short of ninety, he was far too young to die. So he waited.

Past February, when the question of which sandwich he'd like for lunch could make him hang his head like a shamed puppy.

Past March, when the boundary between sleepandnap disappeared.

Past April, when an ambulance stole him from his wife's bed.

Past when he could dress himself, past when he could toilet himself, past when his swollen feet could steady his legs.

Into June, when he smiled only for ice cream; and his wife.

Until July, when even she acknowledged it would be all right for him to leave her.

Elephant's Graveyard

From my father's closet I take two *barong* shirts, hand-tailored from crisp white Filipino *piña* cloth. He wore them as his Filipino friends did, with dress trousers, instead of a suit. I see him standing beneath the stairs of our house in old Saigon, a cigar in one hand, the other in the left-hand pocket of his tux slacks. He is tall, lean, young, his laugh deep with smoke and bourbon. The hem-stitched tails of his shirt move, stirred by the high ceiling fans. My second sister will take the shirts now, along with the red and black brocade vest he wore for holidays. She will remember him handing out gifts early Christmas morning, while I will take his bathrobe, and wear it when I am tired, and pretend I am invulnerable, my father's eldest daughter.

My father has been dead for twenty months. I sift through his clothes, his papers, these pieces of a life finished and ready for boxing. It has taken me almost two years to face this room, this task. Almost as long as he lay dying, twisting in his wasting body like a reptile trying to shed its outgrown skin. I still see his hand move to the cluttered nightstand. I still smell Old Spice cologne on his plaid bathrobe. His life continues in eddies of movement and memory, evoked like some ancestral ghost by my attention to its passing.

On a bookshelf littered with old gun magazines, the *Army Times*, oily pieces of a disassembled pistol, is a red velvet box. The corners are threadbare, the intricate brass clasp bent. Inside are dusty medals: the Bronze Star, with clusters; the Silver Star, with clusters; the Purple Heart, with clusters; ribbons and bars and other decorations tangled together. This one from Belgium, this one from France. This one from Korea, or is it the Philippines? No clippings saved to piece together a soldier's life, to tell the story of a young captain's stand-off at the Battle of the Bulge, of a tall major's reflexive execution of a woman guerrilla. Always they seemed to come first, those nameless men who live on in tarnished metal and ribbon. Two years after his death, I am with him in this small double room as he turns heavily to his side, and I find him watching me once more, and I know that he is—for that brief moment—once again mine.

When I was younger he was seldom mine. He belonged to the land, to the travels he orchestrated like some colonial explorer.

One moment he was home, swinging a small girl with braids high into the trees. And then he would disappear, like an elephant behind the large leaves of the wet forest foliage, slip quietly into some hidden place I could not follow. I would stand still, wondering when he would return to occupy the chair at the head of the dining table, when we would climb over his newspaper-covered lap. When he would remember us, waiting for him at home. Now, he moves ambivalently between here—a high hospital bed with its enameled iron rails and faded, flowered sheets bleached for safety, not comfort—and that wild highland forest, its green heart of palm and poinciana and wild cassava. Sometimes I see reflected in his absent blue eyes quiet, colorless water: the mountain lakes of central Vietnam, the shallow bays of coastal Thailand.

On his dresser is one of his many knives. I remember a yellow pencil in his fingers, how he sharpened its lead with precise cutting strokes. He draws a horse, its neck arched against a military bridle. He draws an elephant, mahout riding high up behind its ears, as large as wings. I take that drawing in my hands as I pick up the knife from his dresser, and I am once again a small girl, needing his attention.

He cannot give it. His mind has slipped that leash. Sometimes I sit beside him still, twenty months after he is gone, dead and buried in the worst Oklahoma winter in nineteen years, watching the way his hooded eyes look inward on somewhere else, some place he knows quite well. I cannot follow him. I remain behind, awaiting his return as I did when I was small. Sweeps of time are lost between his comings and goings, while I wait and wonder what he sees.

He moves restlessly, captive in the bed he once dwarfed, and I think of the way the bright green hills of southern Thailand move like a woman's body under a heavy robe. Of how an elephant can materialize in all its silent, wary bulk, between the teak and the tamarind. Of the places he has been and lived and known. He journeys still on private pilgrimages, secret missions to places with heavy, ancient names—Angkor Wat and Phnom Penh, Chumporn and Câp St. Jacques—riding once again in his olive-green Land Rover over narrow elephant tracks into the greener jungle.

I'm not sure why I watch him fading in and out and in, catching somewhere in between. I don't, often. His absences are easier than his presence. When he is here, teasing his nurse, playing with my sons, it is more difficult, more draining. These are the fragments of our past: the joker, the proud family man. When it is just the two of us, when my mother has retreated to the uncomplicated haven of her room at the other end of the house, he cries, unable to relax within my care. As I roll him to his side to change the soiled sheets, helping him with his BVDs, adjusting his hearing aid, he rails against the enemy that is age and disease. He does not fret the pain; he was never a physical coward, the scarred and tattooed veteran of three wars. He regrets the confinement, the dependence, the loss. He regrets the need for me.

When I was younger we fought bitterly. My sixteenth summer I did not speak to him for three months. We communicated through my mother: "Tell her this." "Ask him that." I hated him for his comings and goings, for his unfettered movements, for our unacknowledged roles in his *hegira*. Nights, I would lie in bed and pray to god that he would die. And now, finally, he lies dying, and I tend his wasted body, sponging oatmeal from silver stubble, wiping an old man's tears from a wreck of a face. While my mother, adrift, cries her not-quite-widowed tears, adrift, I try to bring him home one more time.

Tucked into the corner of a closet are his favourite boots, scuffed elk-hide Dan Posts. I place them in a box for the Disabled American Veterans; no one in our family will ever wear a size sixteen. And I see my father striding the red clay path that winds behind our tile and stucco house in Nakorn Srithammarat, in southern Thailand. The path is only two feet wide; he is almost too large to fit between the mango and banana trees. Under his boot heel he crushes the heads of newly hatched snakes, still coiled in tiny wreaths. They are wet from their hatchings, and curl into their deaths, princeling cobras, he called them. I climb high into the frangipani and watch, my concentration divided between the hatchlings' delicate colors, which dull almost before they blossom, and the finality of my father's heel. The snake hunt is a frequent chore in the jungle so recently carved into a home. From the twining banyan trees I watch as he laughs at my mother's fear of giant tarantulas, as he twists ripe bananas from their stems. Then he grows smaller, distancing himself as he leaves, for that ill-defined work he did, always elsewhere.

As the mental tide recedes, his clear periods shorten. When he is here with me he realises his helplessness. He was never good at helplessness, better always at mine than his. When I was pregnant with my first child he came to sit with me, I confined as he is now, slave to the growing life that tired me. We spoke of my job as a journalist, of the family responsibilities that would soon engulf me. He told me a little of his three wars, speaking obliquely of his choices and regrets. It was a short, precious time, never to be repeated. I realize now, as he looks into the here that is my tired face, that I was still his, even then. Despite the job and house and husband that crowded my time, until I, too, became a parent, I was still his. I did not know until this very moment that my being his mattered to him. When I cooked a meal to feed the two of us, me big with unknown child, him large with known appetite, I was his. When I listened to his stories of men dead since Belgium, of his frustration with the years that undermined his credibility with the victims of this newest war, I was his. And he was mine, as he is for the brief moments he remembers, sliding present time into focus.

He fights, still the warrior, still the anachronism. A Crusader, a Berserker. Now hooded, like some once-fierce raptor brought to wrist and belled. The anger that filled him even larger than his long and heavy frame has become a child's irritability, a mocking echo of passion and power. There will be no shouting matches with dignitaries, no defense of a Korean or a Vietnamese or a Thai soldier against the imperial blankness of a distant government's bureaucracy. There will be lunch at noon, snacks at three, his bath at five-thirty. There will be buzzers, schedules. When he moves into that other, farther place, is he still traveling? Still bribing officials to give him his way? Still dominant and passionate . . . ?

He has lost more than one hundred pounds. The thin-handled spoon moves the gruel into his mouth when I feed him, and he tries to swallow, obedient. His broken teeth are the dark yellow of the elephant's, the large elephants who roam those faraway hills, who know the secrets that link ivory to bone. I wonder if he misses the hot sausage I cooked for him when he could still taste, before his throat was partially paralysed by his latest stroke. I think he remembers, somewhere, cornbread and buttermilk, biscuits and gravy. But now, his 6'5" frame is fragile. Even the wide bones of his jaw and heavy brow seem diminished. As he frets under the light quilt, I remember the man like a tall teak tree, three screaming, laughing daughters pinioned safely within his tanned arms. He cannot lift even his head now. And I, the eldest of those daughters, sit here wondering how much longer he will take to die.

In a torn airmail envelope, tucked into a dog-eared book of Kipling, are some clippings and a couple of faded ribbons. When I pull them out I smell the sawdust and sweat and manure of the stable, where I rode when I was nine years old. He had bought me a horse, an ill-tempered, small-boned bay mare named Pampa. From the bench by the indoor paddock of the stables he would watch me as I cantered around the hard dirt track, a slim pig-tailed girl who thought she was flying. When I took my first ribbon for dressage he was there as well, waving with understated nonchalance as I trotted forward to collect my third place. If his eyes see me, I tell him stories of that little girl and her father. If he frets from burdening, from guilt, from age and the treacheries of time, I sing him the songs he sang when he was tall, vital, young:

Mine eyes have seen the glory of the coming of the Lord . . .

Sometimes he smiles. The smiles are becoming rarer, like the elephants, like the rain forests he knew in Baguio, Chiengmai, Songkla.

It is hard for me to realize he is dead. This is only one more long journey into some new terrain, a longer time elapsed between homecomings, nothing I need fear. It takes me months to realize what I'm doing, that I am still waiting for my father to return.

I catch myself listening for the sound of him, his peculiar shuffling footstep compounded of age and heaviness. I think I hear his phlegmatic cough in the next room. And always I see him looking at me like a ghost from behind my two sons' watercolored eyes. But he isn't there. He will not be a guest at the table when we gather this Thanksgiving. Nor will I soothe him as he starts at some internal sound. I count all the holidays when he was somewhere else, and I remember that this one, and all the ones to follow, will be different.

Because I held him close I am not guilty. Because I changed his diapers, cleaned the ears that once had a price on them, washed him and turned him and fed him and held him through his nightmares, I have made a kind of peace with his absences. My sisters twist within their separate guilts, pierced and pained and angry. I still do not believe he's gone. The peace I gain at his expense extends only backward, into that exotic past where he retreats strategically, marshaling resources for some final foray.

There is no final foray. There is no last glorious moment for a scarred warrior. There is only slipping farther and farther into some other place, watching as he stops talking, stops whispering, stops seeing. And I try to tell myself that he has conquered something, even here. He has conquered death as he once conquered life. And all he had to do was stage that last and final retreat into one of those faraway places he knows so well, moving into the dark spaces with the elephants.

When the bent old men who carry his veteran's coffin hand me the carefully folded flag, I am crying. As I watch my sister, tall and stern in her own immaculate Army uniform, the woman's version of my father's dress blues, I am crying. I am crying as the rifles fire in concert. I am crying as we toss flowers onto the pearl-gray surface of the coffin. It seems that even in my dreams I am still crying. But the crying never helps: it does not tell me that my father is really gone; it does not tell me that he will not wear this *barong* shirt; it does not stop the looking back. Nor do the dreams, in which he comforts me as he seldom did when I was younger. Nor does this final taking leave of his possessions: the fingering of worn metal, the smoothing of starched shirts, the careful catalogue of memory. I set an ivory elephant upon a table and close his door.

From the collection of Britton Gildersleeve, photograph

Letter to my Father[*]

June 15, 2007

Dear Daddy,

Happy Fathers Day!
Not long ago you said you'd been thinking and wondering what you were here for. I said, to take us all to brunch—trying to lighten the mood and shying away from the things we never talk about. You've always seemed a little impatient with introspection, as if it were, if not wasteful or self-indulgent, at least impractical, unproductive.

And often it is. It's also my longstanding habit and part of why I've always admired the discipline with which you keep going forward—not grimly, from a sense of duty, but with curiosity and interest in what will happen next.

So, while I don't know what you feel your life has been for, from my vantage point, it's obvious—and equally obvious how much poorer the world would have been without it. Modestly and without any fuss, you've done good things for everyone you've come in contact with—Mamma, Granny and Grandfather, Brenda, Maureen, Marie, Grandma and Grandpa, Helen, Mary Rose, Agnes, Mary, the Butlers, all your children and their families—and those are just the relatives. You've provided financial support, no small thing, but above and beyond that you've given us love, concern, respect, attention to our individual needs and wants: a sense of welcome in the world. We all know, all of us who have lived in the circle of your affection, that with you here, we'll never be hungry, or homeless, or all alone.

We also know, from watching you, that the world can be a better place than it sometimes is, if only we honor our consciences by living out the virtues we recognize in you. You may not have set out to be a moral exemplar, but you have been, to all your children and grandchildren. Though it looks like a thankless role, all responsibility and little reward, you've filled it gracefully, almost (to use a pedagogical figure of speech) Socratically, more by discussion and example than by lecture. And Socrates may not be a bad analogy here: As Mamma has shown us the power of feeling, you've shown us the power of thought. It takes both, compassion and reason, to form a conscience and every one of your children has developed a strong one, however differently we display it and however short we may fall of satisfying it.

But this all sounds very heavy and your touch has always been light. It takes a sense of adventure (and no little courage) to take a carload of children on vacation every summer, making sure they see something of the world and also get to stay in a hotel with a swimming pool. It also takes a mind and a heart that can imagine pleasure for others, as you did the years when you devoted a special day to each of us, to do whatever we liked best (did you really take Amber to the pro wrestling matches or am I making that up?). As tired as you must have been from work—work you enjoyed, it always seemed, but work often clouded by office politics that wore you out—you kept those dates with us as if you looked forward to them as much as we did.

The last few years have been hard for you physically and emotionally. You've spent most of your life focused on other people's needs, not allowing yourself the luxury of asking what it's all about, and now it feels late and your energy is low and everything takes more effort than it used to. So you may look back and wonder how else you might have spent all these years, what else you might have done. And of course no one else can know what are to you, in retrospect, regrets and satisfactions. But I wish you could see yourself as I see you now: not diminished by age, but distilled, so that all the qualities I love—the wit, the kindness, the strength, the sense of justice, the sense of proportion—stand out, distinct, clarified, essential.

I know we never talk about these things; I'm not sure it's a good idea to talk about them very much or very often. But "never" isn't such a good idea either, so I've written this (an exercise straight out of Dear Abby or Ann Landers, I know, but none the worse for that) because I want you to know how much you mean to me and how much the way you've lived your life—your goodness—means to everyone who knows you.

Love,
Diane

*This letter was written and delivered several years ago when my father, John D. Buthod, was facing the loss of independence that followed giving up driving. He acknowledged receipt—"Got your note—thanks"—and said no more. But he kept the letter and last fall my brother found it among my father's papers. Dad died December 12, 2012, at the age of 93, and my daughter read the letter at his funeral—D.B.

I always called them needle trees

though my father, whom I saw only once
a year, called them evergreens.
Mostly, I remember that they didn't
have leaves, no open hands or lifelines
that could predict a future. That one day
each year when I saw my father, just passing
through like he was, we would pick out
a tree for an imaginary Christmas, the one
we would have had if only he didn't live
so goddam far. I have to say I liked my father,
and liked to see how he had changed every year,
the moustache, the second wife, new children.
The only constant was those needle trees
we would visit. He told me he loved them
because they didn't die. No leafcrumble
each autumn, no false hope again in spring.
He came like this each year until one year
he didn't. Second wife called and told me
about the funeral. How it happened without
me, just like the rest of his life. How he
was buried now on a hillside, stand of evergreens
all around. *He loved them*, she told me in her
I-never-met-you voice. *He loved* you, *too.*
And then we hung up, the phone sharp
and prickly like a pine cone, crumbly
and dry in my stubborn hand.

Beholding

There is a way of beholding which is a form of prayer
—Diane Ackerman

Ingenious, those 26 birds, life-sized &
stiff, golden crown of the kinglet,

the soft background sky, the sudden
paradise of intimacy, the fact

that none of this is life-changing; *it must be
some accidental loveliness*, Robert Cording wrote,

even the world without us
sometimes better, especially

when the red-crowned crane arrive
to their winter-home in the DMZ

and we lift champagne glasses, fluted
& fragile as we sometimes feel.

Yet we congratulate our longevity
in the city of birds, especially

in those last 3 weeks of December
when grief might take

an unexpected turn, when we
might realize that any day—

loose in the world—is as good as our
preconceived idea of paradise.

So, here: *open your hand—receive
this little aftermath, something wild*,

feather descending pale gray
onto your palm, this life

without guarantees, this rare
gift of assembling, of remembering

the first of anything you held,
lovely & amazed,

transient,
your mother's face.

Mark Weiss, photograph

After Words

Mother,
late last night
after I'd uttered the poems,
and you'd risen from the crisp white sheets
to suffuse the room,

I finally forgave your aging
to that ill-jointed,
raveling Rumanian doll
propped on my childhood bed,
staring with faded silk face.

I forgave your dangling doll legs,
your unbelievably silent mouth,
and those worked hands
that don't work, even a spoon.

Finally, I forgave
your enduring—
it is such a Jewish gesture

that I wanted to go
to your third floor, east wing
with flowers so freshly cut
they didn't know they were dying;

I wanted to turn back the crisp white sheets,
release you from all restraints,
and lift your bird-frail body
above my head,
like a Chagall bride.

Trumbull Avenue, 1981

The bounding dog may have been a Dane.
Memory does not retain the breed, save
that his large frame bulged with muscles
and he ran with the happy grace of athletes
beyond praise and blame and score. The sun
hammered that broad anvil of Detroit,
the squinting hookers, the wan wild kids
up from Tennessee, black kids one step
from Alabama, the old Armenian
who ran the cleaners, who still wept
for dead parents and his young bride
seventy years after. As for me—strange
to waken each day into the same life,
or, now, into the sequel of the story—
I stood, half-blind from the cooked
concrete and flashing windshields,
near the burned apartment where a kid
had been killed and others sniffed or
shot or swallowed whatever they could
and fell into some drastic sleep. The dog
came from a side street chasing a mate
or just running from sheer canine joy.
The old Ford was invisible to him
as God's fist. Poised on the ruined hood,
a most sudden sculpture, he died fast.

Detroit Tapestry

At home plate in a bright kitchen I stand
like Kaline, swinging a phantom bat
pointed up, then leveled through the zone;
but I can't run to first, since Mom needs
to open the fridge and a Formica table lies
in my path. On the green diamond above
our yellow kitchen, Jim Pavlinac drives a ball
down the line and against an empty warehouse
beyond the fence. Tall, kind and indestructible,
he rode me on handlebars to practice. His dad
reupholstered old chairs and his withered mom
endured. Somewhat lower in the tapestry
my father fights off men leaping from the dark
jungle to slit the throats of boys left
in his charge throughout hell—having borne
the Pacific war back to a market on Hamilton.
How could it be otherwise? Above our lost
home's heraldry, a gangfight flares,
guys peering around a brick school
with guns long and short. A blaze creeps
from the bottom, not consuming. Flame wends
through all, linking our rages, our benighted
love and work. Once, I slipped
cutting in a roof vent and hung cursing
from the edge, having learned one way
I wouldn't fall from life. Soon we'll careen
wheeled walkers down our stairs and splash
into the basement, losing all record of dads,
heroes, and clutch hits, having borne so much
and braved, two on a bike, such roads.

Simple Syrup

1.
The peonies' plush beauty
has pushed them over;
I need to stake them.

While the first cricket
tries to rush June along,
as if joining our complaint
about the weather: too soon.

Even the dogs won't go out
to help adjust a stirrup,
comb a tail, climb on up again.

My mother died in a heat like this,
air too thick to breathe,
no cooling rain in sight.

I leaned against her on the sofa,
so she wouldn't topple,
dressed to the nines,
awaiting dinner guests,

her head too heavy
for its stem, like those
creamy petals bruised
around the edges.

2.
Our old dog knows
how far she can walk each day.

Sometimes, all the way to the mare barn; sometimes,
only a few small steps from the door

then back to bed, where she sleeps and waits
for every open door, grocery bag, delivery.

Life comes to her now
that she can't go get it,

like the peonies I persuade
to linger in their vase
by putting sugar in the water.

Dear Home

We planted these
three-storey Leylands,
extravagant wisteria,
strung eight miles of fencing,
laid the stone wall.
We are seeds, motes, milliseconds
of light, but also custodians
of clouds and barns,
blades of grass, and handfuls of children.
I walk our fire road,
a dusty metric
linking what was
and will be,
holding me fast
to what we birthed, dug,
hammered and tended.
I look up to see
one brushstroke lighting
the khaki sky with dawn,
in love with something more
ineffable than you.

Letter to my Cousins

Love you all like brothers
—Rosanne Cash

Because I'm listening to Johnny Cash,
remembering our West Virginia summers,
teenagers piling on that old tractor that wouldn't
start unless Freddie straddled the engine, held
the choke with bare hands, me at the wheel,
fourteen driving that baby *wide open* like
it had wings of a T-bird, propelling us down
Fenwick Mountain, Clayb yelling *Go Bessie*.

Because when you built Buster's new barn,
I was your runner replenishing supplies, never
telling you how I got stuck in barbed wire
taking a shortcut across Spencer's field.
And because the trout we caught in Black River,
after a long day in the fields, were the best
I ever tasted. At times we ate groundhog
and squirrel, or some nights, a whole meal
was sweet corn, tomatoes, Aunt Edith's biscuits
slathered with apple butter made in that giant
outdoor kettle passed down for generations.

Because I loved being *one of the boys*, exploring
hidden caves, helping on Saturday mornings
sweep the church, polish pews, shine windows,
and evenings practice hymns, Shirley at the piano,
Buster on fiddle. Because you dove from cliffs
into Panther Creek where we swam near the mines
after church on hot, sticky Sundays, and I would
have drowned if Delmas hadn't grabbed my arm
when the current dragged me to the edge of the falls.

Because we rode forty miles in the back of a pickup
down mountain roads just to watch a drive-in movie.
And because Aunt Pearl called last week—Uncle Thermon

isn't doing well, forgetful most days, but recalls quite fondly
how I jabbed his elbow with a fork when I was a kid.
Because I never told you I carried the heavy ache of leaving
on those long, silent drives back to a quiet home in Michigan,
and because after all these years I still see you together
on a warm July night sitting on the back porch glider telling lies,
the voice of Johnny Cash trailing from the kitchen window,
your laughter rising in that moon-crazed sky.

Mark Weiss, photograph

Maimonides prays

Praise be to God, in gratitude for everything.
Esau still searching for his birthright.
Lily leaves underwater opening and folding,
their languid rotation on their stems.
I open my wolf mouth. In the red-walled cave
of the patriarchs, webs strung from palate to tongue.
Praise be to God for their bones, finally naked,
their shrouds fallen in shreds. Praise for the one
who wraps them in nine layers of carpet.
I come with my blown-glass lantern
from the street where we live like interlaced fingers.
Soldiers are skipping between rooftops,
slipping out windows, the birthright has flown off
like a songbird. Praise for the guttural caw
and its answering silence. When I sat down
at Abraham's table, I was given a loaf
and a small dish of olives. Now they ask,
What did you take with you, out of the City of Friendship?
A pious child who spits stones on the Sabbath.
The soldier who asks, *How small, how tall,*
what did you do? and the soldier who answers,
A small kid with his brother.

A Head Is a Hard Thing to Carry on Your Shoulders

[ANTIDOTES]
Because a soldier guarded a prisoner all night
he could not kill him in the morning
They were boys, really
A poet was briefly intimate with a machine gun
A librarian stole documents. A glazier broke glass
When a partisan beat a prisoner to death
accompanying his blows with *This is for my mamele,*
this is for my papele, this is for my Rochele
his commander neither commended nor reproached him
A prisoner kept a diary so it might outlive him
A poet's mother approached him at the barricade
If he let her in, he would have to let in all the mothers

[A HEAD IS A HARD THING]
I woke saying *Why?* It felt like an answer
I walked and a thought said nakedly
You have misread the dream
the lean years are *the fat years*
Thought always talked like this
A scone or a stone in your pocket
The fat year adjusted its weight
on the chair as it reached for the butter
I stood on the brink with thought
I felt so lean-fleshed
waiting for something to come up out of the river
and swallow something that came up out of the river

[TO CARRY ON YOUR SHOULDERS]
A man sold a blind weaver for ten kilos of sugar
I have heard that need breaks iron
A man got fat skimming the bread and butter rations
Hunger, I have heard, breaks iron
What does it take to remain human?
For some the requirements are simple—
a bent spoon, a shallow bowl
a diary buried with blue-skinned fingers

A man sat at a small deal table
drinking his coffee as sweet as he wanted
as long as the sugar lasted
The weaver's loom was a lyre

From the collection of the Editor, photograph

Pioneer Comfort

In order to render
the moosefat (running low
on soap and candles)
my wife went out—days
after cholera took the baby
—into that damn howling,
each gust slamming
against the barn
like a rabid hound,
to split two logs.

How the night
wailed—you'd think our
trap shattered the paw
of the alpha prowling
for chickens—as my
wife wearily lay
on our big clothsac
stuffed with broomsage,
my lips wetting her
wind-parched nipple.

At Hearst Street House, Berkeley

for Caleb and Demian

Trouve avant de chercher
— P. Valery

It was night. My new life
wandered outside on the sidewalk
in the dark. I watched as it stopped,
stared inside, a reflection in the glass.
Nothing was clear, but I could see
the new shape outlined in the grass
in the rain, going nowhere, hazy, like
moonlight refracted in fog.

Behind me, a yellow lamp,
a child's picture of a many-colored room,
orange and silver and gold. Each wall
a different color. The family slept on.

But something was wrong,
a drop had occurred in the atmosphere,
a permanent change in the weather,
and whatever life I had lived before
I would never live again.

Saturn

Dim, golden, green-ringed medallion, precious
droplet of intangible essence, buoyant in blackness,
it nurtures new green leaves in silent lanes
in valleys. Custodian of woodlands
and bungalows, glimmering through silhouettes
of wind-tossed leaves in the silvery darkness
of bedroom mirrors; cunning observer
low above chimneys and theater roofs; reader
of arcane symbols on warehouse walls; elusive
planet of Clarity and Truth and their attendants,
Intuition, Logic, and Dream; bitter planet
of love unexplored, of a green-eyed woman
with rain-bright hair, seen once on a bus
and never forgotten; scribbler of stealthy light
on dormers and pediments; ambiguous advisor
to girls who must end their first affairs;
guardian of words that a woman said one night
and later forgot, and her husband misremembered;
reedy-voiced singer faint in the distance,
fitful guide to lonely wanderers, consoler
of lovesick boys; volatile governor
of the seven kinds of rain; farthest planet,
embracing all that is, twelfth of the twelve
signs that spell out the world; revolving
globe that accumulates awareness, recaller of lost
brooms and faded rage; rare coin that flits from hand
to hand, slipping, at dawn, through the seam
between ground and sky, vanishing at the instant
when sleepers begin to dream.

The Words We Lack Spiral from the Dark

for Will, from a line by Kim Hamilton

Crossword puzzle, says Richard, pointing to the jigsaw
puzzle Will and I have worked, reassembling Van Gogh's
The Sower, sun setting in yellow sky on purple fields.
Jigsaw, we automatically reply. Though last night,
in the mountains, I looked up at planet Juniper
in a blue-black sky. *Jupiter*, said Will, though names
are hard for him to come by. Frayed, the mind's net
of sound that sings up the world, the cochlea's hair-
trigger delicacy, the tongue's report, the dusty archives.
But not heart's recognition, your face and mine.
Oh love, in the turning years to come may what we lack
be only words and not the heart's intent. And the words—
write them down, across, puzzle-shape; read aloud;
what we mean spiraling up again from the dark ink.

Otto Duecker, *I Love You*, oil on board, 10.5" x 12"

Crow Hours

Always we saw them in the trees by the river.
It was the summer the cutworms claimed

my mother's tomatoes, when a falling turkey oak
shattered our dining room window. The farmhouse

began crumbling around us: dirt caking windowsills,
bricks coming loose. And then the neighbor girl

drowned beneath the green bridge while collecting
crawdads, dust lingering ghostly in July air.

And across the river old men and women always
seemed to be sitting on their front stoops, watching.

And my sister found a bat wedged in the bark
of a shagbark hickory, hiding in full daylight.

Some nights the moon sank so low above the corn
it seemed to founder, gone to shoal, and once

I saw a red fox carrying in its mouth a dead field-
mouse, the rodent twitching until the fox shook

it to remind it it had died. The smell of wet grass
prowled by the cistern where the exposed bone

of evening lined the ridge. And always the crows
had their secrets. Original crows, the darkness

of their wings lifting in air. Formed from rich,
black loam, calling methodically into the conspiracy

of wind, or appearing bitter above us, sharp wings
cutting sky. Sometimes the cries came closer, the feathers

darkly beautiful. And the nights were bruised flowers,
an estuary of moonlight feeding its mouth into

the field: marrow-white, severed, falling bodily
to grass, the hours as permeable as clay.

Solstice

This is as deep into night as you'll get.
This is as out on the edge as you'll be.

Now the small fires of stars burn coldest,
and the owl intones its hollowest notes.

Holiday houselights now shiver and blink
while the wind pursues ghosts over drifts.

Now all the brightness from that far window
falls like an icicle, breaks in your veins

since you are the one outside, passing by.
And although you are already turning

out of the midnight into the glow,
tonight you find no comfort in knowing

that this is as near the abyss as you'll get,
this is as far from the light as you'll be.

Coming in from Storm

> *. . . this flake / That alights on my hand /*
> *. . . making my life . . . / Into . . . the boundless /*
> *Moment of Now.*
> —Yves Bonnefoy

Stamp the boots firmly
by the front door—take no snow
inside but what
now has flown in you—

crystals that have locked
across the walls of the heart—

it listens, listens
in the dawn of ice that has come:

a language, serious, pure,
has been beating there—now you grasp it—
since before your world
was only the mother garden, only the ripe plums, berries
        staining your hands for love.

To live for the snow fallen in the heart
it is essential to stand quietly, alone among winter trees,
seeing how the large fair flakes settle, and stay
only briefest flowers along your dark sleeve.

The Hazelnut

. . . and all manner of thing shall be well.
—Julian of Norwich

This thing: the
plague. This thing: the
earthquake. This: how we
know we must die . . . and all
such "manner of thing" we make
for killing: bombs, fog of
gases, injections . . . . And, then,

such other manner of thing that
we, though dying, are made for loving —
are made for longing always to own:
lovers, children compounded of our
very hearts . . . even silence of a single
summer evening — tangle of white roses
on a worn wooden fence: all such

manner of thing surely loved, surely
to be lost, brought down, torn from their
names, as salt in water loses itself in
a new body that can be only that same
body, only the mystery that is the thing
that is water — Julian, *Julian!* Is this
the last drowning you urged us to
risk past all we can gather ourselves

to know, to be? Where find the place
of such "spiritual sight" as that little
ball, no larger than a hazelnut in your
palm, that is *everything which is
made?* — In me, now, only this
want . . . blind reaching, shadowy
wisps of mind . . . . How trust your

teaching to keep me safe, I leaning —
only as fear, my flesh all a basket
of fear — into that abyss, that depth of
sea bottom, where — under heaviest
waters — you do promise that no "man
or woman" can come to harm?

Geoffrey Benjamin Chew, *White Picket Entropy*, photograph

Blue Skies

to my friend, Helen Ackerman,
who knows and loves horses

Janine had been gone six months when I sold the ranch in
Texas and bought a garage in Northern Virginia. Soon as
I told my mother-in-law, Cora, she called in the posse. I was on
the phone with a dozen relatives, on Janine's side and mine, all of
them trying to change my mind. I said the same thing to each one.
"It's a done deal. The contracts are signed. I'm outta here in two
weeks."

"It's criminal," Cora said, "to abandon Charley. It's too soon.
She's still grieving." She'd have had me arrested if she could've —
sent around the law enforcement officer, her son Gene, with a
pair of handcuffs — just to keep me in Texas. But I wasn't breaking any law. My daughter wasn't a minor. She was 19 and in her
sophomore year at UT in Austin. She drove out to the ranch most
weekends, but that hardly counted as being in my care. Besides,
Charley knew I'd have gladly taken her with me.

"You do what you have to do, Dad," she said, "but I'm sort
of settled in at school, and also I don't want to quit my job." She
was majoring in Spanish and doing volunteer tutoring of immigrant kids. "My little group depends on me, so I guess I'll stay. If
you'll be okay going on your own?"

"I'm sorry to part from you, honey. I just can't stand it here.
Memories are swarming." Everything reminded me of Janine, the
house we'd lived in, the ranch we ran together, the great stretches
of land where we rode side by side every evening — the whole
damned state of Texas was one huge memento. Too many scenes
came before my eyes, worst and most persistent the last one, which
Charley, thank God, never saw.

"You'll come to me for Spring Break, right? It's only a few
months off."

Cora and Roy, her grandparents, would cherish and protect
her, uncles and aunts and cousins would surround her. She'd man-
age just fine, maybe better, without her moping, useless father.

"That's ridiculous," my sister Nancy said. "How can she be
better without you? And you won't get better either by running
away. You're making the mistake of your life, Andy."

"Second mistake of my life. According to you, my first was marrying Janine."

I called her later to apologize. "There was no call for me to drag up old stuff," I said. "I know you're grieving for Janine, too."

"I never said it was a mistake to marry her, Andy. I loved Janine. How could anybody not love her? 'Don't be obsessed with her,' I said. I'm still saying it."

They were opposites, my sister and my wife, Nance a homebody with four kids, and Janine...a daredevil, no denying. First time I set eyes on her, glittering and gutsy, she was competing in a WRPA rodeo in San Angelo, and she dazzled me. *Don't be obsessed with her!* Nancy might as well have said, "Don't breathe."

"So long, Deadbeat Dad," Cora said on the phone on the day of my departure.

"You're taking your horses and leaving your daughter," Roy chimed in on the extension.

"I love you, Dad," Charley said on her cell. "I'll miss you a lot. Be careful." Those were the last two words she'd spoken to her mother.

So I drove off into the sunset, hauling the two horses I'd kept, Jonas and Pal, in a trailer. Jonas was mine. Pal I'd bought for Charley, but she wouldn't be riding without me. Riding was a pastime for Charley, not a passion. In her teens, when we couldn't cart her about at our bidding anymore, she would never go to see her mother compete. I wasn't taking Janine's beloved Firebird. I sold him with the rest. My buyer was thrilled. "Outstanding horse," he said, incredulous at the bargain he was getting. "Mighty sorry you lost your wife. Freak accidents happen in the arena, but maybe she'd have wanted you to keep him." I answered sharpish, "He's a rodeo horse and there's no rodeo where I'm going." To tell the truth, I couldn't stand to see Firebird. He was a big part of that last memory I wanted to cast off. As I drove into Louisiana, I was listening to a John Denver song on the pickup's cd player, changing the words in my mind, "'No days are diamonds, all days are stone, / Gotta make the hard times leave me alone.'"

❉   ❉   ❉

Buying the garage was a sound business proposition. It stood at a busy intersection, Routes 123 and 50 in suburban Fairfax, catching the commuters on their way to and from Washington, D.C. The garden apartments and housing developments round about provided plenty of customers for repair work. Only problem, Fairfax wasn't an area I could live in. Too much traffic, too much rushing and crushing, and where would I keep the horses I wanted to bring? "I'll drive you out to Clifton," the owner said. "Only 20 minutes away, but it's real country." I bought a 15-acre property with a barn on it, and a snug two-bedroom house. I painted and fixed up the bigger bedroom real nice and feminine, ready for Charley's first visit.

When she was applying to colleges, UT had been her first choice. "Don't you want to see some other part of the country, darlin'?" Janine asked her. "At your age, you should be having adventures." "You have enough for both of us, Mom," Charley said. "Besides, I love Texas. Why should I leave?" But I hadn't been in Northern Virginia a full month when she told me on the phone that she was applying for a transfer to George Mason for her junior year. She followed me that summer. Cora said, "You've made her too attached by dumping her." Roy said, "That wasn't fair. She'd just lost her mother." I was out of favor with them big time, but I hadn't tried to influence Charley. She was a clinger by nature, ever since she was little and I'd been her main caretaker, all those times when Janine was off on the circuit. She still wanted to be with her Dad is all.

It was great having her with me every weekend, riding and generally messing about with the horses. I'd ride Jonas and she'd ride beside me on Pal. Monday through Friday, she had dorm-life, friends and activities on campus, and maybe she had a few romances, but if so, nobody serious enough to bring out to meet me. I didn't ask. I stayed out of her business. As for me, during those two years, my daughter was the only company I needed...apart from the company I couldn't have.

Then, just before graduation, she sprang a big surprise. "I'm going to Bolivia for a year, Dad. Professor Perez will help me to get a teaching job there."

She knocked my socks off. "I thought you wanted to teach in Texas. 'Working in immigrant communities,' you told me. There are plenty of those right here in Northern Virginia, come to that. Why Bolivia?"

"I want to see another part of the world."

"Okay, so what about a summer trip to Europe? Isn't that where a lot of American kids go after college?"

"I don't want to backpack."

"I can pay for you to stay in hotels. I can finance the whole trip, a graduation present."

"That's not what I meant, Dad. I think I should try being an immigrant myself."

"But why Bolivia, Charl? Why choose a dangerous place?"

Her class had watched a documentary, she told me, about Indian kids who worked in the mines down there and only went to school when they could. "It sort of fired me. Besides, Bolivia's not dangerous."

Exactly what her mother said about rodeo riding.

※　※　※

A month after I saw Charley off at Dulles, MaryAnn stopped at my garage to fill up one Monday morning. She was going in the opposite direction from the commuters, farther on into Fairfax.

I went out to the pumps to introduce myself, as I always did with a potential new customer. "Smart planning," I said. "Avoiding the morning horde."

"I'm an IC nurse at Fairfax hospital," she told me. "I live in Arlington."

"Well, we're on your route then. Please stop in again."

"You bet."

After that, she came in regular. She had different shifts at the hospital, so it often wasn't rush hour and we had time to chat. Separated from her husband, she told me, with three teenaged kids. She was a big-boned blonde in her mid-forties, a couple of inches taller than me when she wore heels. She dressed conservative and permed her hair, a typical Northern Virginia look, as different from Janine as could be, excepting the hair color. Only MaryAnn's wasn't the real thing. Some other things weren't genuine either, but that took a while to discover.

"Ask her out," Ben, my chief mechanic, urged me. "She's nice, she's good-looking, and she's coming on to you. What more d'you want?"

"I'll think on it," I said.

"You got your own personal dating service here and you never make use of it. Go out with her for an evening of company. What's the harm?"

So he'd been saying for three years. MaryAnn wasn't the only female customer to show interest. Fifty-five next birthday, white hair, more belly than I used to have, but women like me. Blue eyes and a friendly smile I still got, but to tell the truth, I believe it's my manner that draws them. I try to be a gentleman.

As it happened, MaryAnn asked me out. She drove in around 6:30 one evening, still in her uniform and flats, and said she was going to eat dinner at the Sir Walter Raleigh steakhouse in the shopping center across the road. "Too hungry and too tired to cook at home," she said. "It was a hard day in IC. Would you like to join me?"

It would have been downright rude to say no. I had no excuse. The garage wasn't busy, as she could plainly see, and it wasn't far from closing time. "Let me buy you dinner," I said. "My pleasure."

That's how it got started, with MaryAnn pushing, and me dragging a bit, until after a few months, we were keeping pace, and I was starting to think maybe I'd met a woman I could care for, not like I did for Janine, never that, but enough to make us both content in each other's company. She said I was good for her. My home was a haven, she said, from the stress of the IC and being a single parent. She'd come to Clifton a couple of evenings in the week straight from the hospital, and I'd have dinner ready, open a bottle of wine, cuddle with her on the sofa while we listened to music or watched a movie. Usually, she stayed the night. Her kids were 14, 16, and 18, and they were used to her working night shifts at the hospital.

They were not times like I spent with Janine, who had so much energy, too much of the life force, I guess you'd call it, to sit still and quiet for hours. Janine had to be doing, whether it was riding, or dancing, or high times with friends and relatives. I'd been pretty reserved when I met her, but she brought me out a bit. Now I was satisfied to spend quiet evenings with MaryAnn.

In bed, it wasn't fireworks between us, no raging passion. Since Janine, I hadn't felt much desire for sex. But it was enough for MaryAnn. She didn't have great desire either. Often, she'd say, "I'm worn out. Let's just hold each other." Suited me fine.

MaryAnn wasn't going to create any upheaval in my life. I imagined us going on contentedly—for how long, I didn't worry—the widower and the divorcee, who'd each already had and lost the love of their lives.

Turned out, though, MaryAnn hadn't been straight with me. Her husband was big brass in the military, on active duty when we met. She didn't tell me "separated" meant "temporary" until he was coming home to a job at the Pentagon.

"Why'd you lie?" I asked her.

"It wasn't a lie," she said. "We *were* separated. He was in Iraq."

I gave her a hard look, and she said, "I was afraid you wouldn't have anything to do with me if I told you the truth," and tears welled up.

"You were right about that." I broke up with her, on principle. But to be honest, it wasn't hard. She didn't like horses, or country living. She couldn't do the Texas two-step or laugh her head off or come up with sudden plans. And everything she wasn't reminded me of Janine.

She called me a number of times, wanting to make up. "I was going to leave him," she said. "I just didn't want to tell him while he was in a danger zone," and, "I hoped we'd marry eventually, Andy. Please forgive me. Let's start over." What was there to forgive? I'd been just as deceitful when I thought about it. I was more hooked on a spouse than she was, and I had no intention of marrying again. On the phone I talked nice, soothing her, but my last word was always, "No," until she gave up.

"No more," I told Ben, after I told him it was finished with MaryAnn.

"What d'you mean, 'no more'? You only tried once."

"I should've known better than to mix business and pleasure. I'm not dating my female customers from now on. I could get a bad reputation."

Ben put his hands on his hips and roared. "Get out, you old stud," he spluttered, and then, looking over my shoulder, "There's a guy standing in the office don't look like a customer. Looks like a hit man. Hope MaryAnn hasn't put a contract out on you."

I turned around to look through the door connecting the shop and the office. I'd never seen the guy before, but I knew who he was. I was interviewing for a pump attendant and odd-job man, and he was my 11 a.m. appointment.

"Get rid of him," Ben said. "He'll scare the customers."

It's true, Robert looked bad, and I soon found out the reason. When we were sitting in my office, he said, "I have to tell you upfront, I've just come out of rehab. I had a problem with drugs and booze, but I'm clean and sober now. I'm thirty-six years old and I want to get my life back in shape. I go to AA meetings and I got a great sponsor. I can work seven days a week, as early and as late as you like."

Just what I needed to hear, that last bit. Ben's a top-notch mechanic, always cheerful with the customers, but he's married with kids. I can't count on him to work overtime. Myself, I wanted to spend weekends after Saturday noon out in Clifton. I'd just bought a third horse and I was acclimating her. "Appreciate your honesty," I said. "Let's give it a try. Do you need an advance to get yourself a haircut?"

❊ ❊ ❊

When Lydia pulled into my garage one Sunday a year back with car trouble, Robert had been with me eight months and I had no complaints. A hard worker and dependable. He had to be. I wouldn't have kept him for his personality.

"My oil light keeps coming on," she said, so Robert flipped her hood.

"Your oil cap's missing," he told her. "You'd have been in big trouble further along."

Oil had splashed all over the motor and the inside of the hood. "Oh, my God," she said, "I'm going to D.C. to pick up my daughter. I mustn't be late. Can you fix it?"

Robert said, "Sure can," and found her a cap among our spares. He filled her oil tank, knocked on the cap with a hammer, cleaned down the inside of her hood, and she was good to go. Looked at him, Robert said, like he was a hero. Must have been a first for him. "You saved my life," she said.

He told me all this on Monday morning, when I came into the office, bringing donuts and coffee for him and Ben, like usual.

"She's real good-looking, and real sweet. You'll meet her tomorrow. I got her oil cap on order. She's just the kind of woman I could fall for."

"You on something, good buddy?" Ben had come in from the shop and heard Robert. "You sound high. Got Boston crème in that bag, Andy?"

"With her, I'd be 'happy, joyous, and free.'" Robert was looking out of the window. Behind his back, Ben rolled his eyes. Then we both stared at Robert. He'd started to shake. For a second, I feared he was having some drug-related spasm. Then he said, "There she is."

A woman I'd never seen before had pulled up to the pumps. As she got out of her car, she waved to the three of us standing at the office window.

I clamped my hand on Robert's shoulder. "Calm down, son. Drink your coffee. Eat a donut."

"I can't go out," he said. "I'm too nervous to talk to her."

As if I'd let him, the state he was in. "That's my job, remember?"

"Good morning," I greeted Lydia. "Hear you had trouble with your oil cap. Managing all right with the temporary? I'm Andy Mitchell, the owner." I held out my hand. "We should have your new cap by tomorrow."

"Lydia Bronson. I'm so grateful to your mechanic. I was on my way to pick up Tara from her father's house. I might not have made it."

Tara was the kid in the passenger seat, a little mophead of nine or ten, a private school uniform on her. I waved and smiled. She just stared at me, big-eyed, brown eyes like her mother.

"Twenty dollars even with the new-customer discount," I told Lydia as she pulled out her wallet. "Having any other trouble?"

"Not with my car."

"Hurry up, Mommy," the kid said. "I'll be late for school."

"No, you won't, honey." Lydia started to get into the car. "She's never been late," she said to me, as if that was something she wanted me to know, that she was a good mother. "Nice meeting you, Andy."

"Looking forward to next time. Drive safely now. You got a precious cargo there."

"The light of my life," Lydia said. She waved as she drove out.

She was beautiful, Robert was right on there, but way too young for me, early thirties I guessed, and too hip, with that short, jagged haircut, short skirt, and red lipstick. She was closer in age to Charley than to me, and she aroused the same kind of fatherly feeling. I had no designs on Lydia. I can say that with a clear conscience.

✼ ✼ ✼

This was mid-October, a lovely time of year in Virginia. The oaks and maples on my property were changing into their fall colors, a mass of red, yellow, and golden-brown, nature putting on its last, grand show before winter set in. I was leaving the garage early every afternoon, around four, to get in good riding time. Going home to my other, better life was the high point of my day.

I kept the horses outside in fine weather, so when I'd changed into my jeans and boots and walked down to the first field, there they were, my handsome trio, coming up the rise from the brook, three abreast, Jonas and Pal, the two geldings, on either side of Lucy, my new mare. Jonas is a black Morab, Pal a chestnut, and Lucy a thoroughbred, pure silver. Water drops sparkled on their manes.

Soon as they had open space in front of them, Jonas broke into a trot, Pal and Lucy copying him, and they ran about, chasing each other. Jonas and Pal started their kicking and biting play, which always got a bit too rough for Lucy, and she trotted off on her own. She's a former racehorse, but she didn't make the cut. On the track she was skittish, her previous owner informed me. I didn't need another horse. I was just passing a Sunday afternoon at the auction. But Lucy called to me. I foresaw her rotten future on cheap, unregulated courses where they run horses till they collapse. I had to take her away from that no-good drug'em and run'em world. Rigorous training still showed in all her movements though. She'd never forget the track completely, nor ever be rid of the bad memories either. She was a high-strung mix of elegance and anxiety.

She saw me at the fence. "Hey, Luce," I called, bringing an apple from my pocket. She lifted her head, gazed at me with those deep, sorrowful eyes that know things her two buddies don't, and never will. I reached out my hand to show her the apple. "I know, honey, I know, but you can trust me. Not all men are on the make."

Then those two ruffians were bearing down on us, Jonas shaking his mane and whinnying. My heart lifted, as always, for he's a sight to see, well-muscled, broad in the chest, black coat gleaming, white-diamond blaze on his forehead. When he came up to me, Pal and Lucy stepped away a space, giving him first right. Dominance will develop in any group of horses, and Jonas is a born leader. Janine and me had to keep him and Firebird in separate fields, "Or they'll do harm to each other," she said, "and Fire'll do the worst."

Among all those pretty, feisty gals in the opening parade at the San Angelo women's rodeo, I picked Janine out straightaway. She had the kind of looks would turn any man's head, and she was all confidence and poise in her white Stetson, white buckskin jacket, and snug-fitting jeans. Rhinestones on her sleeves and boots flashed in the sunlight and her blonde hair glowed like gold. Her Palomino was mainly white and gold, too, and showed in its prance the same self-assurance as its rider.

I was smitten, but I was skeptical. Right, pretty lady, you have style, I was thinking. Let's see if you have know-how and stamina. She and the horse didn't look like they had the persever-ance for the calf-roping event she'd entered. Palominos are showy, but not always tough, and hers was small compared to the quarter-horses they'd be competing against, and Janine herself maybe a bit too fancy for the real thing, too slender and ladylike. I'd have put my bet on the buxom redhead atop the Appaloosa.

I was wrong. She had steel and spunk in her, Janine, and she'd trained her horse to perfection. They won the event. At the end of the show, when the judges pinned a ribbon on her, the crowd went wild. I wasn't the only one rooting for her.

Later, there was drinking and dancing at the Bucking Bronco Bar next to the grounds. Janine was there with girlfriends, no special guy to prevent me from going up to her. "Congratulations," I said. "Fine work. You sure earned that prize."

"Thanks, I trained real hard to get ready." Her blue eyes looked me over boldly. "I go all out for what I want." She gave me a big, flirtatious grin. "So, are you going to ask me to dance, cowboy? You can two-step, can't you?"

We married a year later. I was 28 and Janine 23. Charlotte was born two years after that. The twenty-one years we were together were the best years of my life, before or since.

❋ ❋ ❋

After we'd got her the right oil cap, Lydia came in regular to fill up, and now and again for other work on her Toyota. Robert was all over her at first. Short of going down on his knees, he couldn't have done more to promote our sign, "Always at your service." He made Lydia uneasy. "Back off," I had to tell him. "Let her breathe." After that, he skulked in her vicinity, a long, dark shadow with no light in him. Maybe he was always that way, or maybe the drugs did it. Couldn't tell you, never messed with them.

We got pretty friendly, me and Lydia, sharing regular chats at the pump or in the office. She was divorced eighteen months. She had a job with an IT company on K Street, but she lived in Fairfax "because it's safer and nicer for Tara. Grass to play on instead of city streets, and no nine-year-old drug pushers. I don't mind making the commute for her sake." She came from Ohio, so she had no kin nearby. "We're in the same boat," I told her. "Only relatives I have are in Texas and Bolivia."

She raised her eyebrows. "Bolivia?"

"My daughter's teaching there, in a special school for Indian kids."

"You must be so proud of her. How old is she?"

We chatted about Charley for a bit. Did she have a boyfriend? Lydia wanted to know. When I said, "Not that I know of," she said, "I don't either. I'm too busy being a mother to have time for dating." I didn't buy that. Her ex took Tara two weekends a month, and she had single-mother friends in her apartment complex who watched the kid when she had to work late. There must be some other reason she stayed away from men. "Too busy" didn't cut it.

When the weather got colder in early December, she brought her car in to be winterized. She dropped it off after work on a Friday and I offered her a lift home in my Buick.

"I don't want to trouble you, Andy," she said. "I can walk. It's only a mile."

"No trouble, I was leaving anyway. I'll pick you up tomorrow, too, when your Toyota's ready."

Driving her home, I probed a bit, to see what was what with her and dating. I was curious is all. Tara wasn't with her, it was her ex's weekend, so I could talk free to Lydia.

"What are your weekend plans? You're off duty for two days, right?"

"Tonight, I'll wash my hair, take a nice long bath, watch a DVD."

"Saturday's your night on the town then?"

"I might go out for a pizza with Meg next door."

"Beats me, Lydia, why you don't date. Your phone must never stop ringing."

"There's not a lot out there for a thirty-three-year-old woman with an encumbrance." She smiled at me. "That's how one guy described kids on MateMatch: *No encumbrances, please*. Meg had to explain. I thought it meant debt or terminal illness. I'm not into dating services, and I'm definitely not into men who'll think my daughter *encumbers* me. I nearly lost custody of her once, right after my divorce, and that made me realize how precious she is. Turn left here, Andy, then left again into the parking lot. Would you like to come up for a cup of coffee?"

Rude to say no, but I didn't want her to get the wrong idea. "Just a quick cup. I have to get home to feed my horses."

"Tara's into horses. She's nagging me for riding lessons. So, at heart, you're still a Texas cowboy?"

As we climbed the stairs to her apartment, I said, "I grew up on a ranch. Took it over after my dad died. I'm more at ease with horses than with cars."

"Does that apply to women, too?" It wasn't the first time she'd looked at me like she did now. It's the look a woman gets when the two of you are hitting it off, and she wonders why you're not making a move.

I just lifted my hands and gave her a big grin. "Like yourself, I'm not a dater."

"Seems we have a lot in common in our situations," she said as she unlocked her front door. "No family nearby, no partner. How long since your wife died?"

"Going on five years."

We stepped straight into her living room. Not much furniture, and what there was had seen better days. Still, she'd managed to make the place look cheery and welcoming, plump cushions on the sofa, a woven throw over the armchair, bright window drapes. Gold, brown, and white were the main colors, like bread and honey.

"And you never remarried."

"Nope, never did."

"Not for want of chances."

"I'm a once-married man, I guess." I followed her to the kitchen, leaned in the doorway while she got the coffee going.

"I'm sorry I don't have wine or beer to offer you. I don't keep alcohol."

"Too early for me. Jack Daniel's is my drinking buddy anyhow."

"So is that why you left Texas? To get away from the hurt. . . ? Must have been lonely up here at first."

"My daughter came soon after. She transferred to George Mason."

"Wow, big transition. You two must be really close for her to do that."

"My in-laws worried she was too attached. I guess they needn't have fretted. Bolivia!" I still couldn't get over how far away Charley had gone. I blamed that GMU professor who'd encouraged her. He didn't have a daughter, I'd bet.

The coffee perked and Lydia poured it into mugs. "Sugar and cream, Andy?" We carried the mugs into the living room. She sat on the sofa. I chose the armchair.

"Were you and your wife close?"

"I've never been so close to anybody, except my daughter. . . maybe. We shared everything. Breeding, training, riding horses, our mutual passion." Only, I never shared Janine's passion for the rodeo, but I wasn't getting into that. Too personal.

"What about your marriage? Your ex must have been an idiot to let you go."

"He'd found someone else."

"So, not an idiot. Insane."

"He had reason, Andy. I was going through a difficult time. I was hard to live with. I had an illness. . . ."

"He should have stood by you then."

Lydia shook her head. "An avoidable illness. I was traveling too often with my job, and there was a lot of stress. Mark asked me to slow down, but I wouldn't listen. It was my own fault. I lost custody of Tara for a while. I got her back a year ago when it didn't work, Mark's new woman and his child living in the same house."

"So he gave up Tara? Great for you, but it don't say much for him. Sounds like good riddance, your divorce. How about that illness though?"

"I'm recovering. No symptoms for nearly a year. I'm being very careful, staying out of stressful situations. . . like the dating pool. It does get lonely. I'd like a committed relationship."

My signal to exit. "You'll find it, Lydia. A woman like you won't be on her own too long. Thanks for the coffee."

"I enjoyed your company. I hope you'll come again. Soon."

"Soon as tomorrow. I'll call you when your car's ready."

As I stepped out onto the landing, she said, "I even go to church on Sunday mornings to stay on the straight and narrow. What do you do on Sundays?"

"I go riding. If God's in the sky, I reckon I can connect with Him better out in the open. 'Course, He spends more time in Texas than here. The sky's bigger."

"Deep in the heart of Texas," she said. "A great place to be, I bet."

❖   ❖   ❖

I had my radio tuned to a country station when I left the garage to pick up Lydia on Saturday at noon. Willie was singing "Blue Skies," and I felt in a blue-sky mood, thinking about seeing Lydia, though it was December, gloomy and wet. She was wearing a red rain slicker over tight jeans tucked into high boots. The slicker matched her lipstick and she looked real striking with her black hair and dark eyes, a bit like that young singer, Norah Jones, who Charley likes. She's a friend of Willie's, Charley said, like she was giving Norah a reference. You can see them performing together on YouTube. I did watch once, but Willie embarrassed me, singing, "I don't want to get over you," with a girl young enough to be his granddaughter.

"So what are your Saturday plans, Andy?" Lydia asked me in the car.

"Home to Clifton after I've finished at the garage. Ride awhile, do barn chores. After that, build a roaring fire and settle in for the evening."

"And when you've settled in, how will you pass the time?"

"Open a bottle of Jack Daniel's. Listen to music." Keep my cell phone beside me in case I get a call from Bolivia…or the hereafter. "All my favorite oldies, Hank Jr., Patsy, Willie…"

Robert was standing at the office window. Out he came, soon as he saw Lydia, showing her all his nicotine-stained teeth. She greeted him real nice, Hello, Robert, how are you, where's your jacket, be careful you don't get sick. As if he was a healthy guy to start with. He had on one of his two washed-out plaid shirts and his thrift-shop jeans. Nobody'd guess I paid him good money. What do you do with your cash? I'd asked him. Can't you dress better? Ran up a lot of debt when I was addicted, he said. My AA sponsor says I've got to pay it all back before I spend on myself.

I sniffed the air around him, as usual. He didn't smell of anything except the Camels he smoked behind the Dumpster. It wasn't what he was putting in but what he couldn't get out. No pride in his person. But Lydia treated him civil, and Robert gobbled up her words, a stray cat hungry for scraps, a coyote whose eyes were howling.

Ben backed her car out of the shop, told her it was in great shape now, ready for any weather. "Thanks a lot, all of you," she said, and to me, "See you soon, Andy."

"When are you going to ask her out?" Ben said after she'd driven away.

"I wish *I* had the nerve," Robert said. "I'm her age. Andy's too old for her."

Ben bust out laughing. "You gotta be kidding. Of all the women who wouldn't date you, she has to be top of the list."

"I'd smarten myself up for Lydia."

"Forget it, old son. Goodwill don't sell the smart would put you in *her* league."

"Don't listen to him," I said. "Get new clothes and quit smoking. She might consider you, if you looked and smelled halfway decent." And I might win the Kentucky Derby. It was pity talking.

"I'm just dreaming," he said. "I got no business dating in early recovery. Not till I got a year, my sponsor says."

"What's AA got against women?" Ben asked.

"Nothing. Same advice goes to them. It's falling in love is the problem."

"AA is against love?" Ben winked at me.

"Addicts have to avoid situations that can lead to a slip. We have to be vigilant. Alcohol is cunning, baffling, and powerful." He was using the voice his sponsor must use, sounding like some born-again preacher. "You can be clean for months—for years— then something can trigger the urge," he snapped his fingers, "just like that."

"So what's the connection with love?" Seemed to me a bit of female company would do him a world of good if he could get it.

"I just told you. It's a potential trigger. Love can go wrong too easy. A woman can let you down, and then alcohol is ready to pick you up…*temporarily*. Dating's a red flag, so don't fucking tempt me, Andy."

"Please yourself," I said, "but watch your mouth. Ladies come in here."

I went into the shop. Ben was working on a Ford Escort. "Don't tell him not to dress better," I said. "Give him encouragement. *Some* woman might go with him. Maybe one of those at his meetings, in the same shape he's in."

"Didn't you hear what he said? He don't need to inflict a woman right now," Ben said. "You're the feller needs a new love. Get moving, Andy. Can't you see special when it's offered?" Then he started up his imitation of Waylon Jennings' "She's Lookin' Good," so loud I had to close the door between the shop and the office.

❉   ❉   ❉

I never would have asked Lydia out, if I hadn't had the flu over Christmas. A real bad bout, it laid me low for two weeks. I got real depressed, stuck on my own out in Clifton. It was a bad December, weatherwise as well as otherwise. My fields looked like the Arctic Ocean, great waves of frozen snow I had to trudge across, sick as I was, to feed the horses. I hired a neighbor's teenage son to muck out the stalls, and he was the only person I saw, not a great conversationalist, Yes, No, and Fine were his three words.

My sister Nancy rang on Christmas Eve. "What's wrong? You sound terrible. You ought to be here with us, Andy, with family to take care of you. It's not as if you have a great life up there.

You ought to come back. . . ." Her theme song. "You're not getting any younger. Something worse than the flu could happen."

"And a Merry Christmas to you, too."

"All the kids are here. I'll put them on," switching to a different tactic. Hearing all of their voices, especially Nancy's grandkids', I did think of her full house and feel homesick. Except, I reminded myself, Texas wasn't home any more than Northern Virginia. Home is where the heart is, and my heart was somewhere in limbo.

At midnight, Charley called. "Happy *crackle-crackle*, Dad. How are you? We're driving to *crackle-crackle*." It lifted my heart to hear her voice. I just prayed Crackle-Crackle wasn't out in the wilds, where bandits and other wild beings lay in wait. We got cut off before I could ask her, Who's "we"?

Christmas Day I lay on the sofa, drinking bourbon, watching TV, sweating and aching. I felt real sorry for myself, tears coming down my face, watching *A Christmas Carol*. Janine and me used to entertain family and friends on Christmas, no stinting on food and liquor. She had love in excess, and I got accustomed to a bigger life. But I had no one to love in Virginia, and that's how Lydia came to mind.

I knew she and the kid were on their own, too. She'd told me it was too expensive to fly home to Cleveland. Did she have enough money to buy decent presents for little Tara? I slipped into a daydream, the three of us around a big fir tree I'd cut in the woods, hung with lights and tinsel, a mountain of gifts underneath, all the stuff Tara wanted, the lacy and perfumy items Lydia'd probably like but were luxuries. It's flu and bourbon talking, I told myself. Don't be duped by the ghost of Christmas past.

When I went back to the garage on the day after New Year, Ben said, "She's been asking about you. Robert told her you'd gone to Hawaii with a woman."

"What did you tell her that for?" I asked him.

"Just a joke."

"I never knew you to crack a joke before."

"Maybe it's a sign of my recovery," he said, and to Ben, "She only asked but once. Don't make it sound like she made a special trip every day," and he hee-hawed like he thought he was a stand-up comedian.

"Sounds like you had a merry Christmas," I said. "Not too merry, I hope."

"I went to round-the-clock meetings Christmas Eve and Christmas Day. Picked up my one-year chip. I can date now, if I want to." That nearly made me hee-haw.

Lydia drove in around seven-thirty. She was wearing a sky-blue quilted jacket over her suit, and the kid was in a curly lambs-wool coat. I went out to greet them. "You two are a lovely sight," I said when Lydia opened the car door. "Like Spring come early. How was your holiday?"

"We had a great Christmas. Santa brought everything on your list, didn't he, honey?" She got out, ready to chat while the gas pumped.

"It was you, Mom," Tara said. "I don't believe in Santa Claus."

"Well, you better," I bent down to look at her through the open door, "or you'll offend me. He's my brother." I stood up straight again, pointed to my white hair and stuck out my belly. That got a giggle from the kid and a smile from Lydia.

I started washing the Toyota's windscreen, making big smiley faces at the kid through the glass and mouthing, "Ho, ho, ho." She made faces back and giggled some more. I guess her and me would get along all right, I was thinking.

"How was Hawaii, Andy?" Lydia asked.

"I never went to Hawaii. Hardly went outside my front door. I was laid up with the flu for two weeks."

She looked over to the office window and Robert watching. He waved and gave her his werewolf grin. She frowned at him. "I wish I'd known. I would have offered to help. It's awful to be sick with no one to care for you. But, perhaps, someone. . . ."

She had such a wishful look on her face, I lost my common sense. "I'd rather have your company now I'm well. Will you have dinner with me on Saturday?"

She didn't hesitate a heartbeat. "I would. I'd like it a lot. Perfect timing, too. Tara's weekend with her dad."

"Whoop de-do," Ben said, when I went into the shop and told him. "You finally made the smart move. I'm proud of you."

In the office, Robert was still staring out the window, though Lydia was long gone. I didn't tell him about my date. Why kick a man when he's down? He might have a one-year chip, but he didn't have a whole lot else going for him, poor guy, hankering after a woman he'd never get.

❈ ❈ ❈

On Saturday morning, I wake to fine weather, and I feel great. I drink a mug of strong coffee and go to the barn to feed the horses and release them at last. Jonas and Pal come out prancing, and it's a sight to see, the way those two race about the field, rearing and bucking, reveling in their freedom. Lucy comes slower, like she's not sure the outside world holds anything good for her, as it didn't, I'm sure, in her past. Her present is a lot better, the opposite life story from mine. In the winter sunshine her coat is nearly silver, like one of them unicorns in Charley's old fairytale books. All she needs is the horn. She stands watching Jonas and Pal cavort. Then, like usual, Jonas comes for her. He's gentle with Lucy, but firm, nuzzling her, nudging her, until she's moving, and they trot down the field to join Pal. Then they all stand by the fence, taking in the sun, nipping and nosing each other, a threesome with no problems among them.

I go back to the house, cook up a big breakfast, bacon, eggs, biscuits, and chop wood all morning in the fresh air, the sky as blue as that quilted jacket of Lydia's. Sunshine is melting the snow fast. Pretty soon, I'll be able to ride Jonas again, and I think, Maybe I'll invite Lydia and the kid out one Sunday. Tara would get a kick out of riding on Pal, perched up in front with my arm around her. "She's into horses," I remember Lydia saying. I know Lydia would welcome my arms around her, too. She believes I'm different from those guys she won't date, which is true, but I do have *encumbrances*—a 20-plus years' age difference, and a wife I haven't got over losing. Tonight, I'll tell her up front, I'm not available for that "commitment" she wants.

❈ ❈ ❈

At The Trading Post in Occoquan, a country band is playing, and after we've ordered steaks and drinks—"Just a Diet Coke, please," Lydia tells the waiter—we have a good time dancing. "You two-step like you're Texas-born," I tell her.

"I do feel reborn," she says. "I haven't danced in ages."

Back at the table, we chat about this and that, and when we've finished our steaks, we get up to dance again. It's a slow song this time, "Seven Spanish Angels," and Lydia moves in close, puts her head on my shoulder. It arouses a warm feeling, but it's tender, not romantic. It reminds me of Charley at nineteen, grieving for her mother.

When we sit down and I've ordered another beer, another Coke, I say, "I got a confession."

She smiles at me, and my heart sinks. Bad opening. She expects soft words, I can see by her face. I can't undo that now, so I plunge right in. "I'm not a free man. There's another woman on my mind. . . in my heart. . . ."

"Your wife, you mean? But you must be ready to move on? Isn't that why you asked me out?"

"There can't be anything like that between you and me, honey."

"Why not? We get on well, don't we? You act as if you really like me."

"I do really like you but. . . you're young enough to be my daughter."

"Is that all that's stopping you? Age difference doesn't matter, Andy."

"I'm not in love with you, honey. I'm not going to be in love with you."

A look comes on her face then that breaks my heart. If I saw Charley look that way, I'd want to know who did it to her. I'd want to go out and punch the guy.

"Lydia, I'm sorry." I put my hand over hers on the table.

"Can we go now, please?"

In the Buick, she says, "I've made a fool of myself. I thought I'd wised up. I thought you were a sure bet, Andy."

"I should have told you sooner, but there's no harm done, is there? We haven't done anything we'll regret, just a nice dinner and dancing."

When we pull into her parking lot, she says, "I don't know what to do now. This is not how I expected our date to turn out. Would you like a cup of coffee?"

"No, honey, thanks. It's after midnight. I'll walk you to your door."

She shakes her head. "I won't sleep. Not in my apartment. Take me home with you. Please? It's dangerous for me to be alone tonight."

"Lydia, honey, I told you--"

"I don't have *dark designs*, Andy. I'd just like your company. If I'm alone, feeling the way I do, I'll be making a run to the 7-11 for a big bottle of Gallo's, and I don't want to do that. Not any more."

I'm surprised to hear her talk about drinking. I thought she didn't, but what's passed between us has given her that lonesome, desperate feeling, I figure. I'm well acquainted with it myself. She puts her hand in mine and says, "I could sleep in the country." I feel sorry for her, and it don't seem right to leave her stranded. Maybe, also, I've had too much to drink myself. I back out of the parking lot.

On the long drive, Lydia puts her head back and closes her eyes. I don't think she's sleeping, but I don't try to converse. All the way, I'm regretting my snap decision. *Big mistake, old son*, my reason is saying. *You'll be sorry.*

"Not a palace," I say, when we pull up in front of my house, though it looks nice, welcoming, with the lights I've left on. When we're inside, I say, "How about some ice cream? We didn't have dessert at The Trading Post."

"How about a hug?" The way she looks at me, I have to put my arms around her. Friendly and quick, is what I intend, but when I reach for her, she kisses me on the mouth, her whole body pressing against me.

It does turn me on, but I'm not going to do anything about that. I unwrap her arms. "I'll show you to the guest room."

"Let me sleep with you. Just sleep, I promise."

She's looking real vulnerable, like Charley when she was little and she'd climb into my arms every time Janine took off on the circuit. But I'm not about to make another mistake, an even bigger disaster than bringing Lydia here in the first place.

I take her arm and guide her up the corridor. "This is my daughter's room when she's here. You'll find a nightdress in the dressing table drawer."

❊   ❊   ❊

I'm asleep when she comes into my bedroom and shakes my shoulder, saying my name. When I sit up, I see she's still in her black dress.

"I just want you to hold me, Andy, that's all." She stinks of alcohol.

"I'm not going to do that, Lydia. I'll take you back to bed."

"I haven't been to bed. I've drunk half a bottle of your Jack Daniel's. My first binge in nine months. Shall I bring the bottle in here?"

"No. You're not thinking straight. I'll make you a decaf."

"In that case, just take me home."

It's 4 a.m. by my bedside alarm clock. "Sure you don't want to try to sleep?"

"I'll wait for you in the sitting room. Be quick."

I pull on jeans and a sweatshirt, find my boots. When I go into the sitting room, she's standing at the window looking out, though she can't see anything but her own reflection, and then mine, behind her. "I'm sorry," she says. "I've really lost it."

"'Course you haven't. Too much to drink is all. Nothing bad happened."

"Well, that's not exactly right, Andy. For you it's nothing, for me it's huge. I fell off the wagon, and soon the coyotes will sniff me. I'm an alcoholic. I just gave up nine months' sobriety."

My first reaction is, No way! Robert's an alcoholic. Lydia's beautiful and smart, an upstanding young mother and business-woman. But then a lot of stuff falls into place, no drinking, no dating, nearly losing her kid, the "illness" she talked about.

"Are you in AA?"

"No, but I sure as hell should be."

In the car, she says, "I won't be coming to your garage again. No hard feelings. It's just too risky."

After that, she's quiet all the way to Fairfax, and by the time we reach her parking lot, I know there's no way to mend the rift between us. We say goodbye very distant, and for the last time if she's not coming into the garage again. I'm out of sorts in a big way, though I did the right thing, I tell myself, on the long drive home. I didn't take advantage of a woman too young, and too drunk. So why do I feel like a jerk?

❖ ❖ ❖

"How did your date go?" was the first thing Ben asked on Monday morning.

Robert was standing behind the counter, looking daggers at me.

"It didn't happen. I cancelled." End of questions. I lied to protect Lydia.

"You idiot," Ben said, but Robert brightened up.

"I hurt her feelings, so I guess she won't be coming in here again."

That wiped the smile off Robert's face. "You just ruined my day. And every future day. Why didn't you leave her alone in the first place?"

"That's what I'm asking myself."

"The good news is, I won't drink over it. Other than that, it's all shit. I'll have to talk to my sponsor."

✿ ✿ ✿

A couple of months later, he tells me, "I run into Lydia every so often. She asked me to give you her regards."

"She's not mad at me then?" So she's going to AA. I'm glad to know that.

"She says you did her a favor. Gave her a wake-up call."

"Where do you see her?" Ben asks Robert.

"Turns out we have mutual friends."

"Oh yeah, church basement friends? Gimme me a break."

"I'm saying no more. I wouldn't have said anything at all, but she gave me a message for Andy." He turns to me. "Change of subject. I've signed up for night school in car mechanics. I'm also planning to go to church Sunday mornings."

"So who'll open the garage?"

"Maybe you need a new part-time employee now I'm in transition."

Since then, he's started dressing better. Got himself a decent haircut, too. I guess he's transitioning into a man a woman might want to date. And I guess that woman might be Lydia. They have something in common. Now *that* I'd never have guessed.

✿ ✿ ✿

Early in May, Nancy asks me to visit over the July 4th holiday.

"I'll think about it," I tell her.

"There's a woman I want you to meet. She's widowed like you. Owns her own hair-styling shop. That's how I know her. She rides, too. You'd have a lot in common."

"Yeah, and she could style my hair for free. Charley's coming back in June."

"So bring her with you. She'd rather be in Texas than Virginia."

"I'll think about it."

❖ ❖ ❖

The horses are at the far end of the field. I whistle and Jonas comes trotting across the grass, Pal and Lucy following. I grab a handful of mane and haul myself onto Jonas's back. Off we go, his walk easy and prompt. When we're through the gate, I give him light pressure and he switches into a lope as the land opens up. No more fences now until we reach the boundary of my property, and as Jonas accelerates into a gallop, here it comes, my guaranteed high. Care, a dragging thing, is left in the rear. It just can't keep pace with a fast horse. This is the feeling Janine and me shared. Only thing, it wasn't enough for her. She had to spice it up from time to time with a dash of danger. She'd still be with me if she'd given up rodeo and settled for a safe high. "There's no such thing, Andy," she used to say, laughing at me. I can hear her laugh.

And I'm not a superstitious man, but I'm getting such a strong sense of her presence, I'd swear she was riding beside me. I can almost see her out of the corner of my eye, urging Firebird to go faster, her hair streaming out behind as she outstrips me, shouting over her shoulder, "Move it, honey!" And I would gallop after her, waving my Stetson in the air, shouting, "Ki-yippee-yi," like a movie cowboy.

The boundary fence comes into sight. As we approach it and I'm about to slow Jonas into a turn, something streaks through the grass right in front, startling him, making him snort and rear. It's nothing, the upset of a moment, and Jonas is steady again, shaking his head as if to say, What the. . .? As I'm patting him, saying,

"Good boy," I look about. Was it a fox, a hare? It looked too big and the wrong color, kind of a rich honey. Surely not a lynx? My fences are secure, but maybe a hole has sprung somewhere. I'll have to come back later and do an inspection. . . *before I sell*, the thought ends. Where did *that* jump out from?

Before I sell can only mean one thing. Back to Texas. "I've given in then," I say out loud. But funny thing, I don't feel defeated. The more I let myself think about it, going back doesn't feel like going backwards. It feels like coming to grips.

As I dismount from Jonas and give him a slap on the rump to send him off to Lucy and Pal, I'm thinking, I was the guy who always had the grip. When I married Janine, her mother said, "You got a wild one, Andy. You haven't picked a peaceful life. But I'm glad for her she's picked a steady feller." Her father said, "Give her lots of kids and cure her of that danged old rodeo." He was dreaming, thinking any man could control his daughter—he never could—but it's true, I kept us steady. Kept my grip on our marriage, our love, her wellbeing. Until that day in Houston at the National Rodeo Finals, going on six years ago. That was the day I lost it. . .

. . . *Firebird explodes out of the chute towards the first barrel, clears it, heads full gallop towards the next. All the fans are cheering as Janine takes him into the tight turn, the one she's done so many times before faultlessly. Something I can't see startles the horse. He loses his balance and falls, rolling over his rider. Cheering gives way to a roar like thunder, like a tornado approaching. Firebird gets up, shaking his head. Janine doesn't get up. The saddle horn caught her in the chest as the horse rolled. . .*

. . . *and I'm rushing out of the stands, shoving people out of my way, breaking through the gate to the arena, running, running. . .* and even though what I was running towards that day was already beyond me, already in my past, I haven't stopped.

❊ ❊ ❊

In the house, I take her photo from the drawer and set it on the night table. Sitting on the bed, I tell her, "I've been mad at you, honey. . . for a real long time. I've kept thinking, if you had let me take care of you. . . if you'd quit, like I asked you to. . . ." Her smile is defiant, teasing. "I'm not mad anymore. I'm coming home."

A weight has lifted, one I'd been carrying around ever since the accident, like that heavy saddle that did for Janine. I'd carted this load all the way from Texas to Clifton, and I'd felt it start to slip off as I listened to Robert talking about Lydia. It was obvious he planned to be one half of that "committed relationship" she longed for and I had refused. He'd do anything for her. He adored her. I saw myself as a younger guy, and I felt a kind of release. It's his time for that, I was thinking. I'd had it, too, and I delivered, like he would. Now I was in a different time.

Maybe there isn't a new woman in my future, not Nancy's hairstylist or any other. Maybe I'll always be a one-woman man, but I can live with that. She'd spread her love around, Janine, and she'd like me to do the same. Isn't that what Charley's been doing? Copying her mother? Only she's taken it as far as Indian kids in Bolivia. I'd settle for a smaller sharing, which would still include plenty of people down there in Texas. I'd buy a small ranch for Charley and me. She could bring out the immigrant kids she'd be teaching. They'd take turns on Pal, and I'd give riding lessons, maybe. Eventually Charley would marry a nice, steady guy, an activist like herself, and have her own kids. They'd come to the ranch to ride, too. It was a future that suited me fine.

※　※　※

Charley rings from Paris. "Dulles on Sunday," she says.

"I'll be there, with bells on. Meanwhile, I got a surprise for you. I've decided to move back to Texas."

"I knew you would, when you got yourself together."

"So . . . I guess you're not surprised. Are you happy about it?"

"I'm ecstatic. I love Texas, too. We're going home." Then my girl surprises me. "I'll be going back to Bolivia in September. I've met someone there. Well, Eugenio is Colombian, so we might . . . We want to . . . I'll tell you when I see you, Dad."

I can only think a few words. I can see them, too, in big letters, like they're printed on a wall: Bolivia. Eugenio. Colombian. Add another word: Life! "Hurry home, honey, and tell me all about it." I'm still learning.

Die Young

Alone on the arete of the Obelisk
having leapt from sleeping-bag before sunrise,
one step, another, a thousand feet of air
how easy to cast off, soar through dim space
flapping puny arms as if evolving wings
passing moons and galaxies on my way down,
naturally—oh shit!—deciding when too late
to take it back, do it over the right way
which I've done in the ensuing 50 years
before my slam into unforgiving scree,
spine-snap, bloody eruption of cranium,
poems unwritten, my granddaughter unborn,
like the tag inscribed on a leather jacket
of a punk blonde resentful on the Muni,
Die Young And Stay Beautiful Forever—yeah,
right. I took one deep breath, set boot-edge in next
obvious crack in white Sierra granite,
pluton pondered deep in earth's mantle, puffed and
swelled like some mysterious intuition
never spattered itself into atmosphere
but crystallizing, cooled under the surface,
hoisted two miles and sculpted into canyons
by individuality of glaciers,
like any life fully, imperfectly, lived,
until I stood on the summit in the dawn.

When Our Guest Makes Breakfast

It's not that I'm bored with toast and jam;
just that our guest has sliced a papaya
for breakfast this morning, and those red-orange slivers,
flushed and wet, lie curled on a plate
in the center of our table, offering themselves.

Just that I'm drawn to his hand on the knife,
the grace of his wrist as he peels and carves;
drawn to this blaze of mango, papaya—
and the speckled green kiwi
he tosses on top like a handful of coins.

Not that I yearned for a taste of the tropics
or favor pulp over toasted rye;
just that—this moment—I cannot resist
the cactus pear on the edge of the plate

that he's pared and opened
and placed within reach of my fingers.

Lush Futures Seem to Await

At one of the homes on a street near ours,
there are seeds in the garden, in the birdhouse,
in bowls on the coffee table.
A man and woman crack them between their teeth
as they watch TV: sunflower, squash,
tiny, pale germs of watermelon.

The woman reaches for more,
as if, biting down, opening shells,
she could ingest the abundance
and bloom.

More seeds, more hulls to dispose of . . .
but, still, no fruit.
She spits out the scraps, jagged, unpalatable,
that cling to her tongue . . . except one,
not yielding to control. That one,
irksome as a recurring thought,
stabs its way down her throat;
lodges like a splinter in her heart.

Over time, from this fragment,
something grows inside her,
sharp, poking—until she tilts
from the effort of containing its push.

When we see her, we taste our own
swallowed shards.
Nothing ever fully discarded.

Contemplation with Doors, Nests, and Music

1.
Unless I latch it, the bedroom door swings wide open.
The one at home swings shut unless we prop it with a chair.

There is no wisdom like the way things swing,
no mercy like the way dawn and dusk come calling us

over and over, the way a body demands to be filled
and emptied. Even today I think sometimes

that the world should pay attention, that my heart
and head ought to meet in the middle, that

the house sparrows should still be sleeping in the nest
with their latest brood. Tom told us last night:

the nest is more dangerous than anywhere else.
If somebody must get eaten, shouldn't somebody live?

2.
Does it matter which door we take? The cardinal sings
Rudy Rudy Rudy, Rita Rita Rita. The path makes

no complaints. I veer off from my last companion
and am alone among the trees. A deer runs ahead,

noisy, almost clumsy, leaving its sign in the wet path.
Deer trails thread off all ways, and I think

of the white-footed mice sleeping in their burrows,
damp but content after the morning shower.

Cicadas in the red oak, dragonflies flirt and fight
above the pond, frogs twang their single notes,

and a line of people skirts the far rim. Their voices
drift back to me, scatter into the breeze and hush.

Would it matter if I gave up my job, found a little cabin
and lived for two years on rice and meal, ignored

my wife and children? Thoreau, Whitman, Dickinson —
bachelors all. I can barely remember being single.

The pond dreams of fire, and bits of its being
leap free at every moment, every glance of sun.

3.
Outside the air is fresher, but every stranger
with an obligation is already growling up Everett Road,

rattling over the tracks, pushing the turns
a little too hard. I want food and coffee

and the last bagel with the last cheese and then
to sit with my new friends, to walk one more time

in the woods, to play my guitar while Bill
riffs around it on fiddle, flute, tin whistle,

while new hills and valleys spring up and fade,
new vistas and forests full of deer and wild turkey,

hemlocks and maple and beech and giant burdock,
bees and bats and earthworms and eagles,

all of it solid and breathing, steaming and singing.

The Body

and if we are not transformed, what is there to desire?
—John D. Caputo

Cool near the waterfall, creek louder than the highway.
Good in the dark, writing blind, everything close

and nothing clear. What else but to dream of another life
among such a roar, so much whelming water?

After dinner my friends talked of spiritual healing, of relief
from nagging pains and torments through a skillful touch,

manipulation of auras, so I told how my knee got sore
and swelled and clicked with every step for three days,

then slowly got better, all on its own. My story was
not well received but I want to trust in mystery,

I wait each day for gifts I don't deserve, I am thankful
for lovely women who have healed me many times

without reiki or acupuncture or even looking my way.
I believe in auras near and distant, and that our souls

are bigger than our bodies. My wife called in the middle
of this, believe it or not, to say she'd fallen off the ladder

cleaning windows and broken her arm. She's home,
not in danger but entirely annoyed, with a temporary cast,

a sling, and a prescription for Vicodin. Don't worry,
she said. I believe and trust she will be made whole,

but I doubt anyone will cure her at a distance. There are
miracles, says Caputo, and there are cheap parlor tricks.

The water roars. I'm almost ready to walk to the rail,
my eyes are getting used to the dark, I am reckless sometimes

but not stupid. The body is more than some clay jar
with a dismal eternal glob inserted. It is to be trusted,

especially when it says *Not too fast*. Nothing
I can't see is going to change my mind. The waterfall

twists and rumbles as I move its way, the white glow
alien, fresh, unstoppable, breaking into froth and magic

every second, coming up stunned and foaming on the rocks
and then hurrying onward as if not changed at all.

From the collection of the Managing Editor, photograph

The Juncture

Everything narrows
into a single glittering plain —
no mountains, no hills, no skyscrapers
or houses built on cliffs overlooking the sea;

juncture of earth and sky,
plane of light and dark,
separates and joins, reaching
out in every direction — nothing
to stop the gaze, to focus the mind,
to bump against or disappear into —

clean of people, of cats,
of soot on windows, of song,
of hymns, stream of years, burn of love,
absence of edge, moonrise, the sound

of yes at dawn — increasing, lengthening,
this deep-rooted curve of ground,
holds, shoulders, uplifts — the seedbed
of its shimmer, nothing in between.

We say we live
without interruption,
as if the cup of what we see
spills and coils through its body

and our minds unblur,
not knowing where it stops
or begins, wake full
of solitude, absence of windfall,
the shuttering of light, the desire
to fasten, attach, anything to anything.

Cell

So what you end up with is maybe a comb
& a toothbrush, some slippers here or there

in a landscape you cannot
account for: you got — how? — where?

though you charted it as best you could
figure out how to yet all still falls away — the solid

parts the bloodian bits; those most close who have
diffused themselves, anodynian but

not to be reached to be asked any number of things.
You sit on the side of the bed & look round

at the residue that used to be you.
There is the question of the body, though,

that remains. How it stirs.
The skin, the breath, the eyes, the hair

Solitaire

to *Mary McGowan*
(74)

Certainly
I am better off than Grandma.
No question of that. I sit
In this throne room my very own room, I am
Empress here among the silvers
& peonies, they may be palms

She sat
In a print dress & hose & a corset
Though she never left the house, her He
Being gone & the rest an Equator bordered by sisters
They had spawned

Out my window wild things bloom
That might delight her, the Saint-Saëns
Part of her I reconstruct from Mother
Who never knew her I know
In the way you piece together
All these shards

Of them am I confected—
Very queer how
It gets better every year:
It keeps at bay to some extent
(She would never say)
Dissolution

The Clock that Fell into the Toilet One Night

As time went on
it was vital to know what the hour was
there in his bed, in his chair, as if
some grand affair, an event with no precedent

would soon be taking place, that he could not miss,
& he began checking at dawn, after breakfast,
during lunch, before it, & all the afternoon,
& as he sat there waiting

for what consecration, what great gold fin;
& supper would come, its bit of cheese & banana,
& bed at last again & a final look
at the little clock that lit up when you pressed it

on a button that he learned to do, awakening
a hundred times a night, to ascertain
where one was: he would haul himself
into his chair & slither

into the bathroom & stare at it there, seeping it
from the pocket of his pajamas
where he cunningly concealed it: the dial glowed green.
He peered at it to confirm that it was later

& later, every time,
& he didn't know how it had happened

Echo Rock

When my daughter was young, my father
built a hut for her on Echo Rock,
the granite mound for which the farm
was named and from which, if she faced
the house, she could pitch her name
and have it flung right back. Made
from barn board scraps the weathered gray
that characterized the foreshortened days
of a New Hampshire winter, it had a single
window facing north and a door that she could padlock.

I hear her still, from the clump of underbrush
that kept her refuge and its secrets hidden,
at the end of a day when it appeared
that she had played contentedly alone.
"Thomasin!" she called repeatedly,
as if there were another of her
and it was time now for them both to hurry home.

At the B Minor Mass

How old was he?
Short auburn hair, that merged into
a perfect beard. Tight jeans.
He was, for me,
as he walked into the church,
all human flesh.

The music began. My eyes kept straying
to where he sat, off to the side,
alone . . .

*Typical, pitiful, true: I could be
his father. Add a wig,
and I could be Bach himself, only minus
the genius: portly, serious, composed—oh,
can't the boy see
beyond that? Can't he hear
the thundering kettledrums, the triumphant
high Baroque trumpet announcing
the arrival of desire?*

Joy in the Evening

That feather on the threshold of my building:
it's been there for two days now, and I'm sick of it.
I pick it up and throw it in the trash. Yes!

The day has these potentials, still. Thank you, Jesus!

Out come my leopard-skin sunglasses,
and off we go, Mavis and me, for our pre-din-din walk.
She's on her leash, and look: the sky is everywhere!

And here comes an old man in shorts,
whistling merrily. He's about my age, and listen,
Mavis, listen. It's the Beatles, "I Feel Fine"!

Eleanor Leonne Bennett, photograph

Mother of Phobia

I sweep porch steps this morning
brooming away what was spun last night
in girders and grids of dread. I dust
between railings.

Behind me you finish your milk, grab
your backpack. Schoolbus idles
further up the block. You pause
at the first step, check my handiwork,
then run. Our ritual.

I search the invisible spaces
kaleidoscope of pristine fear
the barest touch the worst
tingle at necklines igniting
every suggestion of nerve.

What engendered this untaught whimper
that you may never outgrow?

I have considered making you face your harmless,
leggy enemy, much smaller than a penny, that I spy
now sheltered in the ell of a step

or how I might heal you, pointing out her
beautiful brown sister settled between fern
and late Peace rose in her own angled blossom.

For now, I settle for one simple act I can still
offer you: I sweep again, snagging the offending
spider and carry her, bristle-bound,
out back near the maple where I free her
amid leaf fall and an end of seasons,
my own unnamable fear.

Gardens with No Apples

In the new Japanese Garden
at the Huntington, the flowering
trees are weeping. Stricken by insects,
their bark, once smooth as a samurai sword,
oozes a desperate sap. No edge,
no fullness, this is how a promise dies.

In the even newer Chinese Garden,
my daughter and I chance on a Chinese
guide. Quietly, he reveals that every inch
is infinitely planned. Chaos, infinity.
Better to not see too much. Hence,
the presence of subtle frames
to limit the eye's desire.
A rock, a fish, a ripple.
Every sad wave in balance.

The living room belongs to Gabriel.
He growls his toy truck
past trees, shadows,
through every gasp and trickle,
then backs towards a crack in the floor.
Today he is dumping frustration.
Today he is dumping anger, wildness.
We watch from a safe distance.
This is the light garden
called home.

Now, in this infinite moment,
I begin my rocking chair meditation.
I take in untamed backyard trees,
gentle their fierce gnarls.
Then, I open myself through every
crack at once.

Bark beetle time. Chaos
weeping. Opening. Ripple of my
daughter's hand, a grandson's garden growl.

The Yellow Bowl

Everything came from the yellow bowl.

Cookies:
chocolate chip,
gramma's brown sugar oatmeals,
Johnnie Appleseeds,
snickerdoodles.

Magical birthday confections:
Doll cakes,
Train cakes,
Clown cakes,
cakes dripping with roses.

Staples from the pantry
and fridge changed
inside the yellow bowl.

In spring it stirred together
cupcakes decorated as Easter baskets
with bent paper straws for handles.

It swirled anticipation:

liquid peppermint
transformed into a cold
solid as we hard-cranked the freezer,
laughing and celebrating the 4th of July.

For the school bake sale,
it mixed brownies,
held beaters for my brother's first
licks of frosting, toddler
eyes sweet with surprise.
Offered up Halloween candy
to trick-or-treaters.

The yellow bowl
was a cornucopia,
cornbread stuffing for Thanksgiving,
pie crusts, fillings, cranberry salad.

Aromas from the yellow bowl
wafted tasty promises,
visions of eagerly awaited
family gatherings,
holiday fun.

Sometimes it poured forth
funeral casseroles
folded together with sadness,
seasoned with the salt of tears.

It brought comfort in winter:
cabbage rolls, meat loaf,
bread dough rising.

Everything—
from the yellow bowl.

Kim Bultman, *Corn Muffins*, photograph

Layers

for my granddaughter

First, she pokes toy dowel through wooden doughnut.
Later Svea learns to plop the colored rounds
onto the upright stake.

She is young, and coordinated. Parents and grandparents
are certain of her genius, and cheer her
every attempt.

When she fits the smallest ring on top,
larger circles will not pass,
or fall into place,

and she sees there is a certain flow, a right
and a wrong order to things,
or the game is over.

Sorting by color takes longer. We carelessly
call them blue and green and red,
but they are more.

The wooden rings come in turquoise and navy,
olive and forest green,
rose and crimson.

She begins to sense the difference, but has yet
no name for the nuance of color,
thoughts that come later,

as turquoise reflects a calm, but hidden sea,
olive, a bite of earth, and the rose of sunrise
precedes the red scars of sunset.

One

If at first I grasped the concept
I can't recall, the memory lost
long ago, but I must, back then, have learned

or how now do I know one, or two or
more? It might have been a lesson
mother took time to share,

or a revelation, one moment
no difference to me between
one and two, then: one

and one and one, my barely tested mind
racing off with what it had discovered.
Sad, though, that such a momentous

occasion is lost to me now.
One little boy, perhaps still
an infant, discovering one thing after another.

Glenn Herbert Davis, photograph

Confession

for Edward Hirsch

My cousin dashed a mate into puree
— Edward Hirsch

To some it may have seemed an innocent mistake
in reading that you quickly corrected, but I suspect
otherwise. We've all a desire to confess, after all. It's why
the police catch so many criminals. They can't keep
their mouths shut, babble to friends and strangers
and even the cops themselves about what they've done,
then listen as their lawyers argue their clients' rights
were violated, that their statements are inadmissible
because they were never warned they could keep silent
or could have a lawyer present while being questioned.
So your cousin confessed to you, a trusted relative,
after you became curious about her husband's disappearance.
He was a ne'er-do-well after all, an embarrassment
to the family. Still, you felt a terrible burden hoarding
that secret and against your own wishes blurted it out
while reading your poem. Sure, you quickly pretended
what you'd said was *My cousin mashed a date into puree*,
but the confession was done. You couldn't hold it in
one moment longer despite your loyalty to that long-suffering
cousin who'd done so wrong. And think about it: Now the
murderess is single, has a known propensity for killing, and
what if that next handsome date offends her? You understand.
Either way it's a confession you were bound to make.

Kore at eighteen

Actually Persephone loved his loving her,
dark-browed, so serious: it proved something about her
— James Richardson

She was eighteen to his twenty-one, & not in love,
though she loved that he—the baddest pusher
that side of Jersey Street—chose her
as his. This, in a day when boys rumbled
with muscle & fists, armed with brass
knuckles, knives & chains. Those dagger eyes, red-
rimmed with fault lines, laughed with her hazel
moons the night they met, though soon,
inside the dark hour of lounges and storefront bars
she passed his packets beneath the counter
into strangers' hands. Late afternoon,
Kore's mother waited at the station, fearing
he'd kidnapped her daughter to his basement
apartment somewhere in the Bronx,
though reality held the pair in traffic
with a pack of Kools, two colas and chips.
The night he peddled heroin, bashed in a man's face,
threatened to erase another from this earth,
he confessed to Kore, his faith in God,
his belief through prayer all sins would be absolved.
When Kore decided, finally, to say goodbye,
he stormed her door, slammed & banged
to break it in. She sank in a knot to the floor,
hands over ears against curses & screams
as neighbors from adjacent apartments intervened.
Someone called the cops. Now, a lifetime
of seasons gone by, Kore summers herself inside,
watches through windows as leaves pile against
a chain-link fence. Snow banks across a garage wall.
At times, she springs open the windows,
lets in the lawless spin of fall and winter winds.

September on the River in our Middle Age

for Bob

We feel the obscurity of an order, a whole—
And so the Potomac that afternoon held a yellow haze,
its flat gray-green overlaid with the light
of late summer, the trees along the shore
still leafy and expectant.
We had stopped that day at a small
bit of land where we had stopped before.
You told me someone had once named
this little island, mapped it,
this land whose shape the river
is always changing—
You couldn't recall what it was called.

I have wanted to remember how it all seemed.
The sharp, watery smells close to the edge
of the land. The vanishings up beyond,
where the river was a dark swerve, long and familiar.
I have wanted to remember the feast
you made for us—
food cooked on a fire. Chicken and wine.
A great blue heron low along the other bank.
I have wanted to remember watching you
beside the shallow, still river, observing
your aging. The slope of lines
that had not sloped before, the way time
will pull your beauty toward some other time.

You showed me, once, some woodcuts
done by a German artist to illustrate his idea
of *city*. In his 15th-Century world,
he made identical images
of walls and narrow streets and high,
crowded towers to define a concept,
though each duplicated picture was named
a different name:

Damascus, Ferrara, Mantua, Milan.
But I want to say the river was for us
that day not an abstract transience,
but ours. And I want to remember
how the ordinary light diffused
into a too sudden dark —
Though why should night surprise us?
That evening sky may have held its color
longer than it had to —

Still, startled by the change, we had to find
our way back home —
And I remember the way the black surface
of the water summoned us,
though the line of the shore was another
disappearance. The moon nearly useless,
now invisible. And I'd like to understand
how it was when we climbed into the boat.
My own fears, the elation of uncertainty.
The way your patient eye seemed to find
the cut in the land as if by feel.
And the way our paddles were a bright,
shimmering sound in the soundless air.
And how the light of even that lightless night
became somehow abiding, even sufficient.

Serpentarium

Poisonous or not a snake pops when crushed by a car,
the neighbor's car, an SUV hybrid that scaled down still has
what it takes. *What a rednecky thing to do* I say.
The right thing he says, matter of fact, not taking offense.

Rednecky, to make it sound as if he wasn't, quite, and *right,*
not Bill of Rights, e.g., 2nd Amendment, but as opposed
to wrong, as in dumb wrong. If he'd walked up to the house,
got one of his guns, the one pre-loaded with snakeshot,

I supposed, and blown the snake back to paradise, or beyond,
that's what I'd call *redneck.* Either way I was enchanted.
The snake's narrative, like the talking frog's in fact a prince,
or the gun's, or the gun dog's, had found the ideal reader.

We went hunting once, and once was enough. Not the noise
or blood so much, but the evisceration. His dog's nose
for quail quivered like a windsock trying on a breeze.
That poor old dog—now blind and deaf and stiff

and barely able to reach the end of the drive, cross the road,
squat and do its business in my field. I'd watch
and relieved myself to see the deed done despite long odds,
applaud. *Good dog.* I'd just waved to the neighbor, car to car,

and noticed him noticing a stick shaped like a snake lying there
in ambush at the blind dog crosswalk, but sticks don't reflect
and on reflecting I stopped, backed up, got out, and prepared to
bear witness. Watching the tire sneak up on the snake

anyone would wonder what kind of a mess was about
to happen, what kind of noise? What part of the brain knows
deflating a snake couldn't be quiet? The bubblewrap part?
The snake was not unaware and tried to snake away.

The inside of its S slid into the outside. A bright day,
and the copper, no misnomer, shined. By instinct
I'd have veered out of fate's way and by temperament
then thought about it all day and the next.

129

The neighborly thing might be to keep the neighborhood safe.
A snake in the field out can end up baled, waiting to bite
the hand that stacks it. Turns out the treatment for snakebite
is, on average, worse than the bite. First aid?

Remember those kits with razor blades for cutting X's
downstream of the fang marks and little rubber cups
for sucking venom out if you didn't have the stomach to suck
it out yourself, although sucking works better? Forget the kits.

Stay calm. Drive to the ER. They will sit you down
and wait… of course that applies to most anything in an ER.
If the arm or leg starts to swell or darken or blister
they'll give you anti-venom made in horses. Not as easy

as it sounds. Allergy is common, more like your bones cough.
There you are snakebit in an appendage and the cure begins
to kill you, but slowly, like the rack coaxing truth
out of every joint, all your secrets and more, noisy too,

but who has time to listen? My wife's boss killed a snake
for the lady next door. It was coiled on her front step,
waiting for her, letting her know: *one false move.*
Makes you want to sharpen the machete.

At a new clotbuster research pow-wow in Arizona,
they gave us an afternoon off to see the desert.
We drove around looking at cacti and walked around
looking at cacti, some of which are larger than border guards,

and for the finale the guide took out a bag of rattlers,
a bag like a pillowcase, but squirmy. One at a time
they slithered and coiled and rattled for us until
he got bit in the wrist by one of the quicker, meaner ones.

Shit he said. *Shit* we agreed. We looked at each other
and tried hard not to remember those kits and where to cut
and how hard to suck and what if the sucker swallows
in the heat of the moment? He put the snake back in the bag.

Down where it'd be hard not to gather around and hear
its side of the story. *Bad snake* you'd want to scold. *Stay calm*
he advised us. We dropped him at an ER where he knew
they do a nice job with snakebite. The amazing thing

about the desert outside Phoenix is the subdivisions
have lawns and sprinkler systems. Why move to Arizona
if you shave to cut the grass? My neighbor and I shared
a riding mower for years until it died, and then we shared a kid

down the street who started a lawn business and worked hard
enough you knew someday he'd be president of something.
When he went off to a good college his sister took over
and when she left home the next oldest was a little too young

to drive a mower so the mother offered to fill in.
My neighbor said *sure, why not,* you couldn't beat the price,
but I was not ready to let the future President's mother
cut my grass. I might add, although not snaky

and maybe snarky but still on the subject of primal fears
and urges, that our lawn boy liked to kill deer with a bow
and arrow. A Presidential sport for sure. He borrowed
one of my trees for the ambush. You climb up before dawn,

stay calm, and wait. Then his mom rode the mower over
and dropped off some sausage, my share of the proceeds.
You have to be polite when people offer to share
what they killed by guile and their own hands,

and butchered too. Everyone remembers the first time they ate
snake. My father's rule was *no cooked vegetables,*
so when the neighbors back then had us over and the dad there
passed around a platter of slimy cylinders the size of fingers

snake made as much sense as okra, which I'd never seen
or heard of and hadn't seen since until the other day
when it showed up pickled and hors d'oeuvred next door.
We take turns hosting the sunset. I've been looking on eBay

for one of those little brass cannons to let my neighbor know
come on over the sun is over the yardarm. I'd like to send over
a blimp that blinks a neon invitation, and will,
once the price of drones comes down.

His porch has the mountains. Ours has the moon.
I used to moonlight in the ER, and the first time my wife asked
you sure you know what you're doing? I've seen everything
at least once my smart answer...except *snakebite,*

and sure enough the other hospital in town sent us over one.
We get all the uninsured stuff. Boring to watch an arm
not swell. People assume they ought to kill the snake and bring
you the head, for ID, which means a head in a jar

in the conference room where doctors sit around and talk about
who has what and where. Welcome to the clutter.
Donut crumbs. Coffee dregs. Pizza crusts. Fortune cookies
that might remind you, in case you'd ever forget,

the earth is but the frozen echo of the voice of Yahweh.
Whew, my all-time favorite and one reason to eat Chinese
in Cambridge, Massachusetts. I'm the neatnik who arrives
to ward-attend for a few weeks and first thing needs

to straighten up. Lesson 1: *clean up your mess.*
I know firsthand that snake heads float,
at least the eastern diamondback, in lazy circles.
Who could resist giving one a swirl? Experts advise

not to kill the snake that bites you. I agree, unless you can
stay calm while searching and destroying. Looking at a snake
in a jar always reminds me of Boyle's Law. He put a viper
in the jar, sucked out all the air, however they did that

in the 17th century, and proved the volume of a gas expands
as pressure drops. The volume of a snake, like the volume
of a balloon, expands only up to a point. Who knew
there were vipers still in England? Or vacuum pumps?

When we were kids in Miami we went to the *Serpentarium*
near our favorite barbecue place way south on Dixie Highway.
Once was enough. A King Kong-sized statue of a cobra
invited you to stop, against our mother's better judgment,

to give her credit. At 10 AM and 2 PM you could watch
a qualified herpetologist [this was before herpes] extract venom
from King Cobras who standing up straight are almost as tall
as border guards and if grabbed by the neck and choked

will drip venom, teaspoon-sized drips from fangs
that could puncture tires, into glass beakers that looked
scientific. Venom isn't gooey, more spit than sap,
and one of its constituent toxins dissolves clots,

but not as good as the leech. This guy had forearms
like Popeye, he was quick, and he almost made it look easy.
He almost had a perfect record. While waiting around hoping
and not hoping to see him get bit, the tourists would watch

what happens at lunch when day-old chicks were dropped
in the pit-viper pit. My sister still has nightmares.
Our mother claimed the chicks were terminal, fate sealed
regardless, but who or what isn't and we weren't born

yesterday. The euthanasia argument seemed too slippery
a slope. Speaking of slippery the place closed after the tourist
and the crocodile incident. Miami needs tourists,
and a good show would be one of those pythons taking over

the Everglades versus a full-grown Florida gator.
Albino pythons, so you'd wonder how they flourish
in the Sunshine State. One day my father brought home
a baby alligator, a red ribbon with a bow around its neck. Cute?

You could buy them at Woolworth's, baby turtles too,
that was before salmonella. This was a gift from a patient,
a Seminole, before casinos and untaxed cigarettes but not
before the roadside shows featuring full-blooded Seminoles

wrestling giant alligators. We never stopped for one of those
so I don't know if stroking the alligator's belly really does
put it to sleep. I hope so. One theory for the reduced roadkill
on South Florida highways is pythons getting to the possums

and armadillos before the cars. No proof and it may all be
climate change, like everything else. Everyone remembers
the first time they ate armadillo. I could go on and on,
like that snake that swallows its tail. Or the kind that flies off

cliffs and makes a living in the canopy. They leap
into the void, flatten out, except their hearts, invoke Bernoulli's
Law, gain lift, postpone gravity, and don't look down.
Whether you call it flying, gliding, parachuting or kiting,

they get from point A to B farther than flying squirrels could.
Venomous too, but weak venom and small fangs. Either way
the trip begins with a leap of faith. On a similar subject
the staff of Asclepius is entwined by a snake that reminds us

to shed our skin and renew on an annual basis. In other words,
invest in an annuity as soon as you join the workforce,
otherwise lose out on the miracle of interest compounded daily.
At the clinic where I work patients rush in to share their bites

and rashes. Life is dangerous and itchy they want me
to believe, and I do, otherwise who need deliverance?
Not just deer ticks but deer attacks, not only rabid foxes
but rabid bears, not only bats in the attic but their guano.

Poison ivy is the state plant. One lady inhaled some
at a cook-out. Her chest x-ray proved lungs weep.
One lady blames whiplash on her husband who swerved hard
to avoid something he claims was a snake. *Why* she asks

would the snake cross the road? A rhetorical question
because she's sure it was only a stick. She'll be OK
with some PT. He smiles and doesn't take it personal.
The art of medicine, according to Voltaire,

is to entertain the patient while nature cures the patient.
Time cures, but only some of the time.   If possible
give chance a chance. Sooner or later extremes regress
to the mean.   It's not that the gods are whimsical.

Nor the planets nor their moons.   The Greeks let snakes wander
through wards that also served as temples.   Friendly snakes.
This was before Hallmark or e-cards. *Get well soon*
the snakes might say, speaking not only Greek but in tongues

that also taste the air. Those who speak in tongues
and handle snakes and play electric guitars at revival meetings
are casting out the devil. Good luck. Allowing for poetic license,
these are the same people who brought us

rock and roll. If your song argues chorus after chorus
ain't no grave gonna hold my body down the rhetoric
is strengthened by the snake you dance with. Faith comes
in many packages. Condoms too. And the risk that comes

with pleasure. Backroad gas stations, not just the back road
we take through peanut country to the beach,
have condom machines in the men's rooms. You can consider
which flavor while standing there drying your hands.

What does this have to do with snakes? Once a year
I go fishing with a bunch of guys, full spectrum rednecks
almost without exception, to Cape Fear on the Outer Banks.
We stand next to the ocean all day and listen to it all night.

We catch the tide and gather the moon and trust the dunes
and think long and hard about how to fool the fish.
Casting your bait to the wind is one way of trusting fortune.
The fish are lucky it's only me at the other end of the line

because after a few wayward casts I wander off looking
for glass. I have a theory of beach glass based on tide,
picnic traffic, and the rum-sugar-slave trade
that helped make this nation what it is today. My kids think

my taste in glass is something else I need to work on.
If it's glass and on the beach and wouldn't cut your finger,
it's a keeper. Not that I don't take pleasure if it's foggy blue
or something early in the rainbow. At the top of the jar,

pride of place, a digit-sized shard that starts red, goes orange,
then yellow in the tip. Surely from another planet with wind
and tide, beer and soda stored in bottles. A fish bowl
would be ideal to showcase our collection. Fish don't think

the way we do, but they must wonder when shrimp appear
out of nowhere, attached to rigs called *Sputniks*, a misnomer
because what the rig resembles is a lunar landing module.
I used to spear fish. You do things in high school that aren't

Presidential and later on you wonder how and why.
The eel heads and necks poking out from under the reefs
look like the oldest men in rest homes where they are
outnumbered 10:1 by even older women. Wrinkled eyes,

jaws working on something other than a sentence.
A diving magazine had a story about eel attacks, moray eels,
and first aid for eel bites. Step 1: *stay calm.* Step 2:
pry open the jaws. I'd add *with a tool not a finger.* Step 0

would be *don't put your hand in the hole in the first place.*
Fact or factoid: a sea-snake bite kills you faster than any other
snake bite? Not what most people wake up worrying about.
Most people wake up worrying about the health

of their annuity or the mole that may be changing, the one
in the eye, way back where no one can see
except the optometrist who can only see it using mirrors.
He wants me to come back every year for another *retinal map,*

which brings to mind those ancient maps when the world
was flat and had sea serpents waiting for whoever was brave
or lost enough to sail over the horizon. There's always
more than one mole, but one in particular. The eye tech says

look straight at the camera. The eye almost needs to touch
the lens that's looking in. The tech thinks I am not trying
or not paying attention, but for anyone with sunken eyeballs
it's embarrassing how the eye, mind of its own, backs up

out of fear or blinks at the last second. Talk about sunken,
imagine Kafka trying to cooperate. There are eyeball parasites
in Africa that swim in the aqueous humor at the front of the eye
between iris and cornea. They don't look like seahorses,

but they should. More like paisley, but that's true for most
parasites. In our country we just have bubbles floating by,
mostly harmless bubbles. There are parasites in South America
that swim up the urethra, right up the appendage to the bladder,

and once there are not able to back out due to the orientation
of their spines. Speaking of nature's cruelty, can a snake bite
you while it swims? Can they swim under water
and surprise you from below? No. No. Not in a just world.

Except for sea-snakes and that's another hemisphere.
Sometimes snakes have corners. They can assume the shape
of a birdhouse, bluebird houses that come in kits
that make nice gifts, at least people keep giving them to us

as house gifts. No pun. One wall is hinged and opens up
so you can show the kids the nest with blue eggs the size
of white grapes. Sky blue, a deep sky. A hopeful sight.
That's when the neighbor called, this was before cell phones,

and asked me what to do, as if one day at med school
there was a lecture on extraction. His house, from a kit,
was attached to a galvanized pipe that didn't rust or stop
the snake but did pull out of the ground. Holding the house

high, like something you'd see in the revival church
leading the preacher towards the altar, I carried the snake house
across the road and over to my field, shook it out, a rat snake,
let it unkink and de-cube and disappear in tall grass

a month shy of being hay. Field-mice don't keep score
or expect a safe world. Instinct takes over in lower life forms,
but humans—regardless of behavioral genetics claims
against free will—humans are the only species who know

that they know but need to kick it around, think it over,
dress it up in allusion, turn it into myth, digitize it
and Photoshop it and back it up in the reptile folder
on the jump drive. We also have opposing thumbs

and the backache that follows bipeds around.
Two kinds of humans: those whose backs hurt all the time
and those only some of the time. Snakes don't look like
their backs hurt. Speaking of myth: can they hypnotize victims

before striking? Only if the victim has a bird brain.
Can snakes bite after they die, instinct lingering in the puddle
of cold blood, that first gasp of mortality turn vicious? Linger
the operative word. It may be grasping at straws to see

the spark of life as an ember. It may also be mixing metaphors.
If the dunes where we go fishing know where and how to shift
and guard the island from the storm tides that arrive
on full moons and won't stop at anything man made

but get soaked up or worn out or something by dunes
[it's not just the sand, it's the grass too]
then you'd think anything is possible, even Ouija.
In some dimension dunes have to be endless. Chances are

there are five dimensions at least. You'd wonder at least.
When I let the dogs out of the laundry room in the morning
and it's still dark out and no moon, there's a flash of green
that I can see when I'm not looking. No one else can see it.

Hello? Stuff like that you can't plan ahead.
Near the dog food can in the garage a snake has draped its skin.
The dog food brings mice and the mice bring snakes.
They are tiny, necklaces small and clever enough to move

in and out the gap between the inside and the outside,
under the gasket and over the ramp, or disappear
from the corner of your eye through the crack between
the garage and the crawlspace and at that moment

and only at a glance they are in two spaces
at once. Pretty quantum for something that exists
outside Schrödinger's Box. There's the wave theory of light
and the particle theory of light, at least there used to be

back when I took Physics for Poets, and there's the squiggly
theory of reconciliation that no one else believes in.
Where I work I submit a budget that the dean's money people
question and their questions are like those word problems

asking if train A leaves the station at 8 AM heading south
at 40 MPH and then train B down the track starts north
at 30 MPH an hour later, the question is when and where
they meet and what then? My question is couldn't train A

be named something else? The *Orange Blossom Special*
with fiddles for locomotion? Something with heartbreak
and biorhythm. What if a neighbor's son was on the trestle
and had nowhere to leap but down? There was a river

down there with a current and there are word problems
involving rowboats trying to beat currents.
The last time I saw him he and his girlfriend were in full bloom
sitting on a bale of hay in our field and making out

as if all the world's doors were closed, curtains drawn,
oblivious to oblivion, a moment that still breaks
the collective neighborhood heart into pieces smaller
than grains of sand that were already too small

even for the other worlds you mainly find in poems.
His dad used to come fishing but then he moved away
and started over. What scared me as a kid
were not the monster-sized monsters but the little ones,

not the beasts that roared but the ones that spoke,
not the dinosaurs but the snakes, not the snakes with fangs
but the ones who asked you to move close and listen,
the ones you wouldn't say no to, not the lies but the truth.
Its hiss.

Heron & Harp

I drag my harp across the gapped
terrain of pier—a hundred feet with nothing
underfoot but slats of air and swirling tide—

and place the harp in front of me to play
"The Water Is Wide," a sort of joke here,
where the channel is so narrow.

A few notes into the song: a squawk.
Flying low, a heron glides across
the river's edge to land beside me.

Head tucked so his eyes can stare me down
from his perch on a piling—

summoned by the strange cascade of frequencies—
or did he mistake the arching frame for another
large and gawky bird?

I keep the tune going, a slow air
we would call it, as the oscillations rise,
retreat,

then leave song and bird, the harp and me
suspended in a pulse, a wave, a measure
where the water is wide enough
to hold us all.

cemetery

the dead walk at night Tante Icléa said
one November my sister hovered over the Buick
Jimmie who drove said I was unconscious
but I saw her she wiped the windshield with her veil
left right left right looked in on me
the dead walk at night Tante Icléa said
mind you she was buried in Long Island
Pinelawn to be exact but she was there
on Eastern Parkway and Buffalo Road in Brooklyn
she must have just appeared how else?
the dead walk at night Tante Icléa said
though their bodies become bones in boxes
they wander hover stay on the move
How else would you explain:
black dolls calabash bowls
  live roosters dead Guinea hens
    roasted corn smoked herrings
      semen-filled knotted condoms
        bags with soiled shorts
upon the ground of an all-white cemetery?
who is to receive these offerings?
the dead walk at night Tante Icléa said.

Mourning Tom

We end in joy.
—Theodore Roethke

I will do it with splashes
of ochre and orange, alizarin, cerulean
on a canvas as wide as his Huck Finn grin,
a riot of kiwi and turquoise storming
the cliché: desert hues at sunset,
Cape Cod wind and water, wood grain
and tree limb bending to
his sculptor's hand.

I will do it by fusing matchsticks
with glue sticks to sharp sticks, to broken
sticks, to stockade sticks, by building
boxes, by boxing in the light
in bricks of glass that catch
the morning swimming by
like tropical fish in a tank.

I will not tear the world apart.

I will do it by taking the stage
where I can be absurd,
abstract, abnormal,
where I can be an abdomen,
an Abominable Snowman,
a man lost in snow,
a white sock.

I will do it by telling tales
of my Italian relatives,
Uncle Giovanni and Cousin Dominic,
though I have no Italian relatives,
have never been to Italy,
and do not drink wine.

I will come to love hummingbirds.

I will do it by cooking
with every spice on my shelf:
oregano, basil, cardamom and dill.
Cinnamon, mustard, chili pepper, sage.
I will make a poem for the palate,
a prayer for delight. I will mix
and mash and make more than enough.
I will feed everyone.

Connie Bryson, *Hanging Pots and Pans*, oil on canvas, 24" x 36"

Ode to Jimmy Buffett

Of course it's your own damn fault, Jimmy,
or should we call you *James*? You're
a bit long in the tooth for diminutives,
don't you think? It's *James* Earl Jones,
James Taylor, *James* McAvoy—
You could be his *grandfather.*

And sponge cake?! You don't seem like a nibbler to me.
Do you know how many calories in even a small slice?
355, *that's* how many. Have
you ever heard of diabetes, James?
It's nobody's fault?
Denial if I ever heard it, big guy. Even

those lab mice are smarter and buffer,
re? nutritional supplements: bagel bits
soaked in vitamins B and D, ginseng, garlic—
Now that's a feeding frenzy!
It fires up their mitochondrial furnaces.
Listen up, parrotheads:

Rx: three oz. of red wine on special occasions,
i.e., weddings, birthdays, bat/bar mitzvahs,
not gold *and* silver tequila for those
margaritas, those raisons d'être.
You need to change your
attitude in *all* latitudes, JimBo.

So stop blaming that mystery woman;
she's probably spinning on Saturdays,
kickboxing on Mondays and Wednesdays,
caring for her 84-year-old mother blindsided by
Alzheimer's *every* *day;* talk about "wastin' away."

She forgave you for all those wet towels
abandoned on gleaming, hardwood floors,
dirty dishes left languishing in the sink,

never remembering to separate plasticfrompaper,
and saying she reminded you of
your third-grade teacher Miss Plum

instead of Michelle Pfeiffer in *The Fabulous Baker Boys*
whose heart was like a perfectly ripe
pomegranate, seeds like tiny rubies
you tossed in the sand
without a thought.
That was *your* fault, James, your own damn fault.

Kelley Vandiver, Pomegranate, oil on canvas, 12" x 12"

The Visitors

No one seems to be home,
and the note on the door
says "Gone," yet what are words
these days but things
just slung around? Still,
we've traveled such a distance.
If they're gone, it would be
almost unbearable,
not because we love them —
in fact they're hard to love —
but because, you know,
we're the kind of people
who think a step forward
is a step well taken.
Life's too short, we always say,
and don't put off until tomorrow
what you can do today.
We pass these things on — clues
for living well and long.
We suspect they're here, hiding
as they often have behind "Gone"
and "Beware," and other signs
that we know are really saying,
"Find us, please." They're always
sort of lost. And this house
of theirs, this house is weird,
as if it was built with floorboards
that wouldn't tongue, wouldn't groove.
Something about it feels forced.
On their walls is some framed mish
and mash, which they call art.
The door's unlocked.
They don't appear to be here —
closets emptied, refrigerator unplugged,
and a note on the kitchen table, addressed
to us, which they cannot possibly mean.

The Leader

Hypocrite lecteur, — mon semblable, — mon frère!
— Baudelaire

Transparency is not for you,
or anyone
who wants to get things done.

It's for the guy with nothing to hide,
the country
with a hidden wish to lose.

Take sides only after, in private,
you've agreed.

Assume everyone is holding an ace
up his sleeve. Play yours
after you've perfectly rolled up

your cuffs to show it wasn't there,
perhaps after
you've railed against deceit.

The people you're dealing with
will understand.

Let everyone see what you think
they need to see. Call for a vote.
Enable democracy to lean your way.

History for Ambassadors Or Butterflies and Other Chingaderas

for Domingo Luiggi

Behind every semicolon they scent danger. They fear the silence between stanzas. In East as well as West they are certain that when in an intricate context windfall fruit is mentioned (quite incidentally), it's a dig at them . . . But we writers are indestructible. Rats and blowflies who gnaw at consensus and shit on the newly laundered tablecloth.
— Günter Grass, *Headbirths, or, The Germans Are Dying Out*

Prologue

Mahler composed to free the sway of dark feelings. Picasso painted to rid himself of an indigestion of green. Neruda's creatures were born of a long rejection. Kafka wrote to exile the bugs; Vargas-Llosa, to exorcise the demons; Cortázar, to neutralize the nightmares. Exorcism . . . catharsis . . . the removal of *alimañas*, of vermin. If to write is to be an exterminator, then I will hunt, expose, and deflate *alimañas*. Get rid of that little pain whether in the chicken coop, in the pit of the stomach, or on the behind.

On Amtrak, aided by the romantic spell trains have always held over me, by the motion, or by the three hours to myself, the boil finally burst and overflowed. I had no paper, but the urge to write was as uncontrollable as retching. A brochure. "For Ages 50 to 74. Guaranteed Life Insurance. $1.00 a week. You can't be turned down! No medical exam — no health questions." Over, below, and between the red and blue promises, around the geriatric smiles, and through the iconic cherub, my scribbles.

The Plot

Actually, the idea was born out of a very small, almost insignificant, incident. A tempest in a teapot. Although, to be honest, it would be more accurate to call it a tempest in a tequila cup. One of those small clay cups with a handle and a floral design on the outside, and a one-ounce capacity. It looks like a toy cup. Little girls can use them for their tea parties. Gringo tourists who want to mimic Mexican machos buy them for drinking tequila. But if it's so small, why bother writing about it? Well, you know what mighty contests rise from trivial things. It's usually the props that start wars, sink ships, inspire epics, and change the course of history, from that luscious red apple that started the whole affair, to Samson's tresses, Salome's veils, Cleopatra's asp, the chalk circle, Celestina's feather mask with a center of dead ants, the glass slipper, the purloined letter, the rape of a lock, the horse traded for a kingdom, all the stolen embroidered handkerchiefs, the lost keys, the compromising billets-doux. In this particular case, it was the license, the non-existent marriage license. A non-existent marriage license? asks Domingo. How can that . . .? Yes, I answer, but please remember that this was not just any ordinary marriage license, not even any ordinary non-existent marriage license, but *the* marriage license, the one that could have, probably would have, changed history. At least it would have changed 500 years of Latin American history. After all, if a butterfly stirring the air in Peking . . .

The Characters

Collar that Dormouse. Behead that Dormouse! Turn that Dormouse out of court! Suppress him! Pinch him! Off with his whiskers!
    — The Queen of Hearts,
    Lewis Carroll, *Alice's Adventures in Wonderland*

The Ambassador. She wasn't really an Ambassador, but she would be, she would be, never fear, she would be.

The Princess. She was the Ambassador's four-year-old daughter. She was cute. *Muy linda*. The entire court doted on her.

The Vice Consul. He had official duties. Young. Needed to please. Knew his job was to be the Ambassador's echo.

The Aide-de-camp. Carmen (not Bizet's, don't get excited). But she did look as dark and sultry as the other one.

The Paramour, a.k.a. Toadie. He was Carmen's paramour, not the Ambassador's—hers had been left behind in Europe, once he had fulfilled his procreative duties—but he occasionally served the Ambassador as escort.

The Knaves. There were two. One carried the Ambassador's crown on a crimson velvet cushion; the other was always blowing three blasts on the trumpet and unrolling the parchment scroll.

The Ladies-in-waiting (gentlewomen, attendants) and their consorts. The ladies we will know as a unit, for they acted as a unit. Their role was to accompany agree, smile agree, knit agree, lunch agree, exalt agree, tea agree, plan agree, party agree, flatter (she that loves to be flattered is worthy of the flatterer) agree.

The Esquire. Handsome with an Emiliano Zapata mustache he twirled with his left hand. He was new to the Consulate. He wanted to please, but he represented the law and had to observe protocol.

The Cultural Attaché. *C'est moi.* That is me. That was me. I mean I, us, *yo. Soy yo. Fui yo.* There was a Vice Cultural Attaché, but he wasn't available much of the time. You can't blame him. He was a busy and important academician. So the cultural work fell on me. Not that it was an important official position. I was not a bureaucrat of the Mexican Foreign Service. It was a volunteer position. I worked gratis.

Prelude

Once upon a time there was a woman named Leticia — Leticia, if only her name were Patricia. Whenever her name is mentioned, one hears strings of Bernstein's "Maria" in the background, you know, the one from *West Side Story.* Hey, maybe that's what this is, a *West Side Story,* a soap opera, a *telenovela.* Her name should have been Patricia in remembrance of her cute little nose. She always had trouble with history, and facts confused her, so once she heard in Mr. Morales's class "patrician nose," while sitting in the back admiring herself in her Christian Dior compact, she had forevermore associated in her mind patrician nose with small and cute. Her deepest desire had always been to be considered patrician, especially from the moment she saw *The Robe* with Victor Mature and had her first puppy love crush on Richard Burton, the Roman noble who for her epitomized patrician, high class, aristocratic, ruler. Yes, high class, ruling class, and faraway places. Exotic places like Paris, Milan, Rome, London, Singapore, Miami, Hollywood. Any place, except that tawdry little town where it had been her bad luck to be born.

The Wait

La historia oficial latinoamericana se reduce a un desfile militar de próceres con uniformes recién sacados de la tintorería.
— Eduardo Galeano, *Memoria del fuego*

After serving her country in several major European cities, she was assigned to the City of Brotherly Love. Used to a large entourage and a life of music, champagne, elegant women, handsome men, brilliant parties, she was at first disappointed, deeply disappointed, especially because she had thought it was time for a promotion. She had always served with distinction. She had been to all the right places, known all the right people. Could it be because of her daughter? She didn't regret it, no, how could she? But, nevertheless, perhaps if she hadn't? Had her defiance gone too far? The Service knew she had always been free and independent, and it had accepted this. But a daughter without a husband—was it too much for Mexican society to accept? Philadelphia was, in comparison with her last post, so small-townish, so drab. She would have to wait for her ascension.

In the meantime, she would create her own court. She invites her cohorts, gathers her ladies-in-waiting around her, convenes her courtiers, blows the trumpets, cuts the ribbons. No occasion is ever lost. She never misses an opportunity to send an invitation, open an exhibit, say a few words, grant an interview, put her country's name forward, get her picture in the paper, wear a new dress. An artful intriguer, she knows how to seduce the men. At different moments, each feels he is the chosen one. Special individual invitations—to champagne brunches in her penthouse to say thank you for a job well done. What none of the courtiers realizes is that they are all just dessert, window dressing. The real work is done through her feminine *estado mayor*, her unofficial cabinet, during those little lunches at Girasole's, for fair is foul, and foul is fair and her ladies speak a language of their own; can read a nod, a shrug, a look, far better than a printed book; convey a libel in a frown, and wink a reputation down. After each meeting, they ask, "When shall we meet again, in thunder, lightning, or in rain?"

In the meantime, she would play the roles, the roles that had stoked her imagination since childhood. Alone in her penthouse, she pictures herself in various Paris ateliers trying on the clothes and the personalities of her idols.

Some mornings it is Marie Antoinette. She wasn't half-bad, and besides, the guillotine stands right next to Boucheron and Dom Perignon as one of the great inventions of French genius. "Let them eat cake," or "Off with their heads." She could say that with feeling in a long white Carolina Herrera number. And she would ask the director to make sure that the afternoon sun over the Seine would reflect off the gold braid of her dress. The cost of the braid would not be that much either, what with all the cheap labor available in Taiwan, Manila, Singapore, or in the *maquilas* of Chihuahua or Monterrey.

Other days it is Carlota. Empress has a better ring than The Honorable, Her Excellency, Her Eminence, Her Majesty, Her Holiness, or even Inquisitor General. The white dress she wears in the portrait that hangs in Chapultepec is gorgeous, as is the crown. The castle itself offers many possibilities, and the carriages, and the parties, oh, the parties she could give at The Castle. To rule over an entire nation, and to have a beautiful husband, a real European prince. And, besides, Empress is the title that best suits her. But wait, hasn't she heard something about a firing squad at dawn on the Cerro de las Campanas, and Carlota in exile and mad? And wouldn't that be a betrayal of the PRI, of the official, the institutional government party? If Marina's son had only been the legitimate one, there would have been no need to invite Maximiliano and Carlota to rule Mexico. There would have been no Porfiriato, no blind admiration for everything French, no blind envy of everything American, no Revolution, no million Mexicans killed between 1910 and 1920. No PRI. Wait. Wait! What do you mean, no PRI? That's a heresy. Wash your mouth with *lejía*, with pure lye. Where would Mexico be then? Where would she be? Who would tell her what to do, what to say, what to think, what facts to spread, what truths to promote. But, if the flapping of a butterfly's wings . . .

Queen Isabella? Give me my robe, put on my crown; I have immortal longings in me. The rumored affair with Christopher was of prurient interest. Was it true? Ferdinand was handsome, but why else would a woman sell her jewels to pay for an expedition? Certainly, to play Isabella would mean power, glory, beautiful costumes. Isabella revived the medieval *hermandad* and placed the Spanish Inquisition under royal control. She was responsible for the expulsion of the Jews, the wrenching of Granada from the Moors, and the discovery of the New World. A smile spreads across her face. If she played Isabella, hers would be the power to scuttle the voyage of discovery, to prevent the colonization, to erase Cortés from the picture, make sure he never appeared in her-story. Oh, but the gnawing doubt. If Cortés had married Marina, Martín Cortés, the first Mexican, the first Latin American, would have been the *primogénito*, the legitimate one, and the other, the other Martín Cortés, the son of the wife—in her version, divorced, renounced, or never married—would have been the bastard, *el hijo de la chingada*, and then we would see how secure the Spaniards and the rest of the Europeans felt, then we would see who had a problem with *chingaderas*, who was on the defensive, who shied from analysis and self-criticism.

Oh, but Eva, the original Eva, age cannot wither her, nor custom stale her infinite variety. The ultimate power trip. The simplicity, the elegance, of the props: a tree, tall, leafy, deep green, graceful, majestic. A snake, long and sensuous. And The Apple. Don't forget the apple. Red, shiny, luscious. But who could design a fig leaf that would disguise her pear shape and compensate for her short legs? And who could play Adam? Robert Taylor, Rossano Brazzi, Pedro Armendáriz, or perhaps someone young, one of the young bucks, what's his name, the one in *An Officer and a Gentleman?* Yes, that one. She could demand that Richard Gere play her leading man. He would look good in an Armani loincloth with all the fuchsia, lime green, electric blue, and touches of gold that characterize his designs. Yes, playing Eva would be the ultimate power trip: with only the red apple and her wide, swinging hips, she alone would determine the future of the human race. And, if either Adam or the snake decided to talk, she would impose restrictions, accuse them of negativity, censor them, and issue an edict: No disagreeable word shall ever be uttered in my kingdom.

Leticia's avatars were all sisters under the skin, or at least under the Givenchy. They were kindred spirits surrounded by the same aura. Regardless of the costume, you could always make out the outline of a crown, a coronet, a miter, or a tricorn hat on top of the strawberry blonde curls, and where they dreamed of holding a scepter, you could always make out the handle of a guillotine.

Divertimento

Do you know the Consul from one of the smaller Latin American countries, the one in that building on Chestnut Street? One autumn afternoon, the secretary from the law office across the hall from the Consulate told me *sotto voce* and giggling how several times each afternoon the Consul walks down the hall toot, toot, toot, farting all the way to the bathroom around the corner. She seems unconcerned about anybody hearing her, totally oblivious to the secretary or the attorneys in that office or the people in the other suites. When the secretary told me the story, she said she couldn't believe that this very ordinary-looking and obviously coarse woman could be a personage, somebody who was sent here to represent her country, someone who buys designer dresses and goes to receptions and shakes hands with Presidents and Ambassadors. She admitted that she had thought that people in high positions had more dignity and refinement. That poor South Philly secretary will never again believe in the importance of high class, titles, or position. The toot, toot, tooting down the hall has forever ruined all auras for her.

First Act

... invitación a la riña y al trabajo, epígrafe del amor, signo del nacimiento, amenaza y burla, verbo testigo ... resumen de la historia: santo y seña de México: tu palabra: ... chingada, pirámide de negaciones, teocalli del espanto.
— Carlos Fuentes, *La muerte de Artemio Cruz*

Such as it was, the first act took place one December evening in a suburban house in some eastern city. Let's say Philadelphia to make use of its history and etymology. It was a tempest in a tequila cup. I said that the Indian Princess Malintzín was Cortés's mistress. He named her Doña Marina and treated her with respect. She was his *lengua*, his translator, and she gave him a son, but when the moment came to marry his Spanish fiancée, he gave Doña Marina to one of his captains, who married her. But the first mestizo, the first Mexican, was the son of the conqueror and his mistress. And we all know what that means. If there was no marriage license, then all Mexicans are *¡unos hijos de la chingada!* Sons of the Great Bitch! Leticia turned purple with rage. She knew she had to act, accused me of heresy, and called for an auto-da-fe in her penthouse. After all, she is the Benefactress of the Arts, and she knows it isn't true that Cortés did not marry Doña Marina. Or if it is true, then it is her duty as a good Mexican, as a member of The Party and as a representative of her country, to deny the truth.

Yes, one of her responsibilities is to promote the culture of her country. And she loves doing that. She loves culture, never tires of saying it. One day she asks who Pacheco is. She has never heard of José Emilio Pacheco. On another occasion, she wants to know if Elena Poniatowska is anti-*priísta*. Somebody has mentioned that she is against the *Partido Revolucionario Institucional*. Leticia has seen her name in the papers. Very alert, very interested. Nobody can accuse her of not working hard for her country, of not promoting its culture. Of course, she suspects that Octavio Paz was a *malinchista*, a foreigner-loving traitor. After all, didn't he say that Mexicans are not strong in self-criticism? The temerity of him! And now, it turns out that she says, that the cultural attaché claims, that Paz even dared to say that Cortés did not marry his Indian mistress, Doña Marina. Imagine! How irresponsible of him. And how irresponsible you are, *tú eres, yo soy*. That could hurt Mexico's re*putation*. A Nobel Prize winner a traitor? Yes, the Consul has heard about the prize, but still, you can never be too careful. And now she says, *yo digo*, that Paz even had the audacity to write all that disgusting stuff about the WORD, *La Palabra*, the six-letter word, you know. Leticia cannot bring herself to say *esa palabra maldita*, that damn, that cursed, that odious word. Paz called it the Mexican word *par excellence* and studied it as a noun, a verb, an adjective, an adverb. Someone else told Leticia that Carlos Fuentes did the same thing in one of his novels. And now the Cultural Attaché has said the WORD in public, at a cultural gathering sponsored by the Consulate. She said *CHINGAR!* She said it. I said it. I said *Chingado*, the fucked one. I said *el Chingamás*, the Father of all Fuckers. I said *el Chingaquedito*, the quiet fucker. *Yo lo dije. Dije chingar, chingado, chingamás, chingaquedito, chingaderas, hijo de la chingada, chinga a tu madre.* She said. I said. *Yo dije chin, chin, chin. ¡Basta!* Enough! If you don't stop sedition, it will spread. The censorious consulette is in a furious passion. She will certainly not allow the word, *la palabra*, or the lack of a marriage license, to be discussed, or even mentioned, in her presence. Off with the tongue of anyone who dares say it in front of her. Off with her tongue! Oh, off with my tongue! *¡Mi lengua!*

Not literature, of course, but she does like the other arts. And she believes in promoting culture. After all, she is the Benefactress of the Arts. She promotes lunches at Girasole's, she promotes dinners at Tequila's, she promotes receptions at the Union Club, she promotes fundraisers in her penthouse. Yes, she is a major benefactress of culture. And she is very careful to enclose all the information, including newspaper clippings with her picture and copies of all the invitations she has sent in the previous thirty days, in her monthly reports. But she will not have anybody disparage her country, not even a Nobel Prize winner, and certainly not that upstart Cultural Attaché who had the gall to give an entire presentation about Octavio Paz and his ideas about the psyche of the Mexican and the Mexican word *par excellence*. The Consul called for an auto-da-fe in her penthouse.

Intermezzo

En suma, la cuestión del origen es el centro secreto de nuestra ansiedad y angustia.
> — Octavio Paz, "Los hijos de La Malinche," *El Laberinto de la soledad*

Scientists who study chaos postulate that in a system of space-time of cosmic dimensions, predictability is perhaps impossible to achieve. All events—however imperceptibly—are interrelated. Other people extend Edward Lorenz's butterfly effect, a metaphor for the sensitive dependence on initial conditions, or the rapid translation of tiny differences in input into overwhelming differences in output, which postulates that a butterfly stirring the air in Peking today can transform storm systems next month in New York, to other questions, such as the contingency of history. If the flapping of a butterfly's wings can transform storm systems on the other side of the world, is it preposterous to wonder what effect a marriage certificate might have had? Might it have transformed the psyche of one-hundred-thirty-million Mexicans or even of four-hundred-million Latin Americans? My country right or wrong. *México lindo y querido, si muero lejos de ti* . . . .As American as motherhood and apple pie. Boys don't cry. *Los mexicanos no se rajan.* Boys

157

will be boys. Blondes have more fun. Jingoism. Cheap patrio-
tism. Domingo calls it *cultureta* and says that the better he knows
Mexicans, the more he realizes they are not very different from
his Puerto Rican compatriots. Underneath the differences of the
various *culturetas*, are all Latin Americans basically insecure about
their birth? How about the Dominicans, Panamanians, Cubans,
Colombians, Chileans, Argentines, and any of the other bastards
of Spain? If Cortés had married Marina, would we all be secure
and able to produce, analyze, and enjoy a living culture that is part
of the human culture, instead of desperately trying to hold on to a
cultureta, a crummy little imitation of a culture?

Second Act: Auto-Da-Fe

*I would like to inform all the intrepid Muslims in the world that the author
of the book entitled* The Satanic Verses, *which has been compiled, printed
and published in opposition to Islam, the Prophet and the Koran, as well as
those publishers who were aware of its contents, have been sentenced to death.
I call on all zealous Muslims to execute them quickly, wherever they find
them, so that no one will dare to insult the Islamic sanctions. Whoever is
killed on this path will be regarded as a martyr, God willing.*
— Ayatollah Khomeini, February 14, 1989

The Knave of Hearts, as usual, carries the Consul's crown
on a crimson velvet cushion. The Knave of Spades raises himself
on tiptoe and blows three blasts on the trumpet. Then he unrolls
the parchment scroll. The Vice Consul and the Princess are ornamented with hearts. The courtiers are ornamented all over with
diamonds. The ladies-in-waiting, smelling blood and responding
to an uncontrollable, ancestral urge, reach down, open the baskets
that appear on the floor next to them, take out the red, white, and
green skeins and the long bone needles, and begin to knit. Some
are already relishing the smell of burned flesh, others look forward
to the sound of the blade. Where have we seen this before? Is all
writing just a repetition? But, wait, there is a difference. Next to
the knitting baskets the Aide-de-Camp has placed pitchers of a
thick brownish mixture that the ladies pour into clay mugs and
sip. Can it be? We move closer and take a whiff. Yes, yes, they
are definitely *jarros de atole*. All afternoon the ladies alternate sips
of the corn mush with the frenzied movement of their fingers, and

slowly the red, white, and green stripes grow until, gradually, one is able to make out a cactus, and later, an eagle with a serpent in its mouth, in the center of the white stripe.

The *hermandad* smiles and nods ostentatiously in agreement with words she has not yet uttered. Of course, they know what she is going to say. The Cultural Attaché boxed her ears. Nothing important, but as we well know, all looks yellow to the jaundiced eye. And if a butterfly stirring the air in Peking . . .

Heeled, coiffed, and Givenchy-clad, resplendent in her full consular regalia, Leticia struts into her living room to preside over the tribunal. A squeaky voice is saying, "What does it all mean?"

"Hold your tongue!" says Leticia, turning purple. The ladies suspend their knitting. The rest are lying on their faces, and the pattern on their backs is the same as the rest of the pack, she cannot tell whether they are her courtiers or other guests. She orders Toadie to turn them over.

"Consider your verdict," says the Vice Consul.

"Not yet, not yet," whispers the Esquire.

"Herald, read the accusation!" says the Vice Consul.

On this the Knave of Spades blows three blasts on the trumpet, unrolls the parchment scroll, and reads:

> For Alice is a traitor.
> She reviled our reputation.
> She said Marina was Cortés's woman.
> She said there was no marriage license.

"Scandalous!" shout the ladies while their fingers knit even faster.

> For Alice is a traitor.
> She reviled our reputation.
> For Alice is ill-spoken and obscene.
> She said *chingar*, with all its conjugations and
> declensions.

"Scandalous!" echo their consorts.

> For Alice is disruptive.
> Her rumors are rebellious and seditious.
> For we all know they are not true.
> For Alice is intrepid and a traitor.

"Collar the traitor. Behead the traitor! Turn the traitor out of court! Suppress her! Pinch her! Off with her tongue!" yells the Consul in her purple fury.

"Consider your verdict," the Vice Consul says to the jury.

"Not yet, not yet!" the Esquire hastily interrupts. "There's a great deal to come before that!"

New to the Court, he thinks that they don't play fairly at all. "They all quarrel so dreadfully," he reports later, twirling his Emiliano Zapata mustache, "one can't hear oneself speak — and they don't seem to have any rules in particular; at least, if there are, nobody attends to them — and you've no idea how confusing it is . . ."

When she does not understand, *cuando no entiendo*, he tells me, *me dice*, "My notion is that you have been (before she had this fit) an obstacle that comes between her and ourselves and it."

"Hush! Hush!" says Toadie in a low hurried tone, looking anxiously over his shoulder as he squeaks.

The Esquire dares to whisper that it isn't important. The Consul turns crimson with fury, and glaring at the dissenter like a wild beast, screams, "Off with his mustache! Off . . ."

Alice says, *yo digo*, I say I don't agree, and the Vice Consul yells, "Let the jury consider their verdict," for about the twentieth time this afternoon.

"Stuff and nonsense!" says Alice, say I, loudly. "The idea of having the sentence first!"

"Hold your tongue!" says the Consul, turning purple.

"I won't!" says Alice. *Yo digo.* I say?

"Off with her head!" shouts Leticia at the top of her voice, looking at her, *mirándome*, with fury. Nobody moves.

"Who cares for you?" says Alice (she has grown to my full size this time). "You're nothing but a pack of cards!"

She's immediately suppressed by the officers of the court. They have a large tricolor canvas bag that ties up at the mouth with red, white, and green strings. Into this they slip the miscreant, head first, and then sit upon her. Through the canvas I can hear someone whisper that there hasn't been a trial.

"Hush! Hush!" says Toadie in a low hurried tone, looking anxiously over his shoulder as he squeaks.

Holding with her left hand the crown that keeps slipping over her strawberry blonde curls, while brandishing her scepter with her right, in her hoarse purple fury Leticia yells, "No, no! Sentence first — verdict afterwards."

Hotel Carmen, New Year's Eve

The hotel carries its grace, its history. Let's down
its chandeliers. Half the bulbs are shot, in their
tipping paper hats. But the glass-mirrored sphere
spread with tinsel ribbons floats like a planet,
suspended for this evening over another year.

Over the buses, late from Juárez, running south
since dusk. Over the small restaurants outside
nameless towns, alone by the highway, their all-
night *parillas*, stacked plastic chairs, chipped
Formica counters, broken metal tables, their *mole*,
chuletas, tacos, carne deshembrada and beans.

Who remembers but the spheres, cycling, as they
have for eons, your first meal at 1 a.m.: how it tasted,
the fourteen-hour ache you'd held in your gut,
half-chilled Modelo from a bucket on the floor,
thirty drowsy passengers stumbling from the bus;

all of us now lingering over our *cerveza*, Cokes,
adovada and chicken, the soaked paper plates, over
one last bite from a last stripped bone, one last sip
from the can still turning in your hand, over
the napkins stained with grease, the toilets
with no seats or paper, over the printed timetable

you could now throw away; the uncapped driver
snoozing in his chair next to the *patrón*, who, on
his bench, now snoozes too. Two women at a sink
washing silver, scrubbing pots. Putting away
the pans. An old man mopping the floor. While

a girl in an apron slowly stirs soup, *sopa azteca*
for the next arrival. With the grill still sizzling,
the burners still blue, our bus still running, parked
out by the road, somewhere in Chihuahua,
headlights, taillights, every light on. Like

the sky tonight, with its tinsel, all its shining planets
sparkling in their orbits, over the new year
now turning to its routes; over the leaping dog
suspended in mid-flight; over us all, waiting
to re-board, the lit-up, idling, Chihuahense bus.

Hayfield

They say it's all illusion, this season turning
as Vicente turns bales in his late August field,
as the cottonwood, overnight, have gone
from green to gold, the air from constant heat,
mornings close to frost. Perhaps it's not
the earth, or the poles in new alignment,
or the sun veering past its summer border;
perhaps it's not the girl, now a woman, who
writes you from your sleep, wakes you again
as autumn makes its passage, the clock
in Mona's kitchen ticking with the kettle,
the simmer-aromatic slow steep of beans
filling the cafe, as it has for ages, in such
familiar fragrance, in such intoxication
you forget the countless years, the long-sold
paintings, your re-soled shoes, you forget
Linda's photographs, her cats, her recent-
decades lover, you forget your own thick
glasses, the loose skin on your arms; you
forget how loose you weren't—as free
as a bird—when her breasts were deep
as smoke, her smell pungent as chile, her
arms for you, even now, as open as a child's.

Twenty Eleven

1
Well, then, if the psalmist defined
   our lifespan as threescore and ten,
   did the crapshooter rolling a seven
think of it followed by zero
   and foresee he would cash in his chips?

   Whether he thought his winnings
were tokens from cloud nine, who gives
   two loaded dice? On day one
he was a squirt in his mother's womb
and will return to eternity's egg

   as "Gramps," who, on weekend jaunts
to casinos in down-and-out zip codes,
tried hard not to step on his shadow.
   If predestination half-led him,
   why shouldn't things after death

lead him to limitless freedom?
   The sun antedated his doldrums,
   and so will the digitized scan
of his grimace survive the time-outs
   he punished his kids with. Their bedroom

   was musty and boring
as an assisted-living ward
   where seventeen riled golden-agers
   waited for nurses at daybreak
to bring pills in small plastic cups.

2
Socrates lived to be seventy.
   In an olive grove he brought up questions
   that flustered his quick-witted students
who strolled and spoke slowly beside him.
   He gave off such green, leafy light,

piercing his prison guards' armor,
that even when they could be bribed
   to let him escape he believed
he would please the sun god Apollo
if he stayed in his cell to serve Athens.

Old age had produced enough numbness
and awe of the underworld's dark
deeper than all oil lamps snuffed
   that he grabbed hold of the cup in both hands
and washed down its hemlock like wine.

So why not commit an Anne Sexton?
   It's the right day to do it: outside
the lobelias are ruthlessly blue.
The geraniums spilling from pots
   are blood-red as suicide pacts.

It's time for the final synopsis:
yesterday's losses at work,
   tomorrow's routines in retirement.
   I limp past a lamppost, my leg
not up to speed for the race.

3
The night I dreamed of a woman
   more than a hundred years old
   I kissed her crow's feet and her laugh lines.
I addressed her as *Melocotón*.
   "No, call me *Durazna*," she quipped.

"My nickname is Peach. I was born
in Michoacán, not Madrid,
   when Mexicans pitted their fruit
   with machetes, not cute paring knives.
Emiliano Zapata handpicked me,

   Pancho Villa seized me by the waist
   and swore he would feast on my soul.

I am yours for this evening, Señor.
  I give you my bulletproof word:
very few poems stay young."

I woke in a Holiday Inn
  with an ink spot of drool on my pillow
and my grandson astir, our TV
tuned to the end of a film
  in which a white-haired professor

  dreams of a day at the lake
where, led by a woman named Sara,
  he glimpses his folks far away.
  Wild strawberries garnish their picnic
at a summer retreat south of Stockholm.

4
Now smack in my seventieth summer,
  I fish for a riddle: Who goes
on four legs in the morning, on two
at midday and on three in the evening?
  The answer is child's play, friends.

  You guessed it in grade school: a person's
a person no matter the age:
  crawling over a carpet, upright
  in an office, or hunched
over a wood walkingstick.

  Well, then, here's my birthday story:
an old man approaching a house
appears to arrive at its doorstep.
  He has gambled on wangling fame
  and building a palace inside,

but the front porch and swing seat suspended
  from chains that are screwed to the ceiling
  keep their distance. They dwindle
the closer he comes, while the voices
  of people he can't recognize

unsettle the silence with "Uh-oh!"
and "Hey, look at *me*!" It's as if
  he's back in a playground with trees
  and blossoming shrubs in the park
  when he was a seven-year-old.

From the collection of the Editor, photograph

Век-заложник

Век-заложник, каинова печать
на устах и на раменах.
Можно всё взорвать и опять начать,
Можно всё, но убивец страх . . .

Я хочу, я пытаюсь сказаться, но
вырывается из горла хрип,
как из чайника, выкипевшего давно
до нутра, и металл горит.

This Hostage Age

This hostage age—the mark of Cain
on every lip and shoulder.
It's possible to shred everything and start again.
All possible, except fear slays everything . . .

I want, I am trying to say, but
only a wheeze escapes my throat
as if from a kettle boiled dry
leaving only hot metal.

Translated from the Russian by Danielle Jones

The Long Walk*

Long shadows

play at the edge of vision
begging remembrance,
"Do not forget us.
We are the darker-skinned sisters.
We, too, made the long walk."

Long nights
dark and cold
dredge up nightmares
of marching
and soldiers
and keening
and quick roadside burials
walking and dying side by side
embracing for warmth against winter wind
sharing slivers of shade in summer
coming into this hard land
working it side by side
midwifing crops and babes

Our relatives have learned well the lessons of dominance,
lessons of blood and broken promises,
and cast us out.

We, too, made the long walk.

———————————

*On the Cherokee Nation's breaking the treaty with Cherokee Freedman

Vse smrtno

Za Neda Rorema

Tvojega mesa, Cocteau, sem se na smrt prestrašil.
V sekundi bi me požrl kot kako
belo ping pong žogico,
spil iz Mitteleurope kot osso-bucoč
in me sesral,
kot si sesral *(chier)*
ton Orphée.
Le da se ta štorija ne bi dogajala pri
Marie Laure, Vicomtesse de Noailles,
ampak v tvojih sosednjih prostorih,
samo za las
odmaknjenih od prvih,
ki še danes smrdijo po zapranih brisačah.
Ves ta čas,
odkar mi je Hélène Martin–Chauffier,
ki sem ji bil zaupan,
ker je bila iz tako trdnih in konservativnih
krogov,
pokazala tvoje okno,
čeprav je zares govorila o Colette,
chose légitime,
chose tres humaine —
sem te smrtno sovražil.
Rabil sem druge pijače,
indijanske bobne,
pecivo iz mormonskega sladkorja,
ki sem se ga preobjedel v Salt Lake City,
redki puščavski zrak,
Georgio O'Keefe,
sand dollars, ki sem jih
sam nabral ob valovih Pacifika
in jih potem pometal z jetov
med miljo širokim in razkošnim smehom
Kalifornije,
večno pobožno strmeč v topo prežvekovanje

živine med baročnimi hribi,
jadri v Devinu,
da sem te,
Mitteleuropa,
napikal s sijajem in ti odsekal klaustrofobično
glavo
s pipcem.
Rabil sem ta *loop*,
ta *détour*,
da lahko nežno razmišljam
o tebi,
čarovnik —
ki si tako sovražil to besedo —
o tvoji smrti,
najvišji solidarnosti do drobne prijateljice
z raskavim glasom,
imago,
ki si za finto odnesel v grob svoj ogenj,
ogenj velikega mesta,
lepa vešča,
sveti duh vseh naših premikov.

Tout Passe

for Ned Rorem

Your flesh, Cocteau, scared me to death.
In a second you'd swallow me like
a white Ping Pong ball,
drink me up from Mitteleuropa like *osso bucco*
and shit me out
as you shitted out *(chier)*
ton Orphée.
Only that this story wouldn't happen at
Marie Laure, Vicomtesse de Noailles,
but in your neighboring places,
a hair
removed from hers,
even today smelling of unwashed towels.
All this time,
since Hélène Martin-Chauffier,
to whom I was given in confidence,
as she was from such a firm and conservative set,
showed me your window,
although in fact she talked about Colette,
—*chose légitime,*
chose très humaine—
I hated you.
I needed other drinks.
Indian drums,
sweets made of Mormon sugar,
which I overate in Salt Lake City,
rare desert air,
Georgia O'Keeffe,
sand dollars I myself collected along
Pacific waves, and then threw from
the jets between mile-wide sumptuous
Californian laughter,
eternally and religiously staring into blunt rumination
of cattle among baroque hills,
sails in Duino.

That I, Mitteleuropa,
stuffed you with shine and cut off your claustrophobic
head
with a clasp knife.
I needed this
loop, this
detour,
that I can think of you with tenderness,
wizard —
you hated this word —
about your death,
about supreme solidarity to your tiny friend
with a rough voice,
imago,
who as a joke carried into graves your fire,
the fire of the great city,
beautiful moth,
holy spirit of all our motion.

*Translated from the Slovenian by Michael Thomas Taren
and the author*

Girl on a Bike

Don't call it an awakening. It was more like a warm spell in a cold winter,
or a flash of color in the green, a goldfinch on a curious flight.

It was in my twelfth year when those attic rooms had door handles
I kept turning but would not open. All those doubts stored within.

But one night it happened. She appeared coming toward me. I stared,
flushed in the moment, only my interfering mind saved my embarrassment.

It creates an ideal, so unreachable. But I was there the next night to see
her come by in that summer sundress. I chose to ignore the mind's override.

I wanted to sit at Fellini's table; even if I couldn't touch I wanted to gaze on
all the round full fruit. With a garland around my head, the gown's

flowing silk on my inner thighs, I wanted to gulp the wine of excess even
if I wasn't sure my mind might rob me again.

One night I decided to see her up close. She couldn't miss me. Those legs,
the freedom under the muslin, pushing, bending, her body swaying.

No one knew about my guilty stirrings. Like a Hopper female, she looked
straight ahead as if I wasn't there. I should shrug and laugh it off.

But chin stubble, pubic hair were gifts to the flesh. The lips of the soul
so often miscast in candlelight, pucker for the taste of plush grape.

There are no prayers for abstinence nor hymns of obedience. Its appetite
needs no permission, makes everything on the table within reach.

Crease of Light

It's a look we all know, when love has left a house.
Eyes once open to the world are squint shut.

The sun finds no crevice, weeds reach carelessly,
blossoms die in infancy remote from nature's breast.

There is no word for this in the lore of the Irish.
Roofs may rot with wind and rain but in the earth

and rock walls is the genesis, rebirth and rebirth.
So the house stands against the bulldozer of reduction,

a spirit to be remembered but we have to leave a window
unshaded and a door slightly ajar.

James Andrew Smith, oil on panel

To Learn from Light

Afterward, waking early.
Dawnlight waiting for the sun.
Planning how to be, rooting
with a rusting trowel in the
autumn garden to unearth
a plastic soldier and it
was November, leaves scrambling
down the naked branches, sky

effaced by a cloud field and
the cold in spurts. Beyond, the
world arrives alone on the
parkway and the tally of
the telephone masts slipping
singly and the wind that slaps
across the grass, across the
sycamores lifting one by

one like stones that sigh into
water as souls rising as
they do, in the season of
not being; we have only
all we remember in the
largeness of the dawn passing
not before nor now but then,
breathless, unattended, new.

Waking

Evening and the faces of the
sunburned trees that circle to the
back of the house and that nearly
begin again in the sky and
a spray of birds gusting across
the lines of color and I can
smell the oak in the new dark, new
night in old places nothing but

one silence on an old one that
brings me to where I'm standing where
once we saw leaves sink before they
touched ground or where in winter we
watched snow flicker before it reached
the ground and was gone like a night
sound unadjectival finding
its own silencing standing where

we stood to find my way back by
going to the last place where I
saw forever sometimes going
to the last place where I stood when
the world belonged to big wet flakes
unfurling and sliding new and
blank before remembering their
way to earth like sleepers waking

A Terrific Headache

Anna brought Lucy to the White House
when Eleanor was on the road.
This father and daughter conspiracy
was a family secret.
Others in the know were committed to silence.
My parents knew. They never told me.

My father was visiting the President for dinner at Warm Springs.
Before that last supper, he steadied the trembling hand
of his long-time boss and friend
as he mixed Bourbon Old Fashioned cocktails and nibbled caviar,
a gift from the Soviet ambassador.
Four ladies were his guests.

Cousin Laura Delano, with her dog. She had never married,
her gray, deeply blued coiffure sported a shaved widow's peak.
Dowdy Daisy Suckley, another spinster and distant cousin,
a Hyde Park neighbor, and more, gossip would have it.

And then there was Lucy Mercer Rutherfurd.
Slipped over from her Aiken estate with artist, Mme. Shoumatoff.
Lucy had commissioned a private portrait of her beloved.

The next afternoon Laura called Eleanor at the White House.
The President had fainted and was carried to his bed.
She was not to be alarmed.
To prevent rumors from flying
Eleanor had kept her date to speak to the ladies at the Sulgrave Club.

Summoned to the phone, Press Secretary Steve Early
"very much upset asked me to come home at once.
I did not even ask why. I knew in my heart what had happened."
Later, Laura would tell her
that in her absence Lucy came to dinner
at the White House, more than once,
hosted by her only daughter, Anna.

Her bitterness and sadness remained private:
"He might have been happier with a wife
who was completely uncritical," she wrote.
"He had to find it in some other people.
I was one of those who served his purposes."

On that final day in the Little White House in Warm Springs,
insulated from the cries of war,
the Commander in Chief, posing
in his favorite Navy cape,
put his hand to his temple.
His last words, "I have a terrific headache."

Ron Pokrasso, *Tree, Dog Right*, monotype, collage, intaglio,
drawing on paper, 16" x 20"

A Sunday in Purgatory

A voluntary inmate immured
in a last resort for seniors,
there are constant reminders that go with the territory,
the grim reaper is ever lurking just around the corner.
I am at home, very much at home,
here at Ingleside at Rock Creek,
cushioned with a safety zone of three miles' distance
from my caring daughter and her family in Cleveland Park.
At Ingleside, a faith-based community
for vintage Presbyterians, I am an old Jew.
But that's another story.
I'm not complaining with so much I want to do,
doing it at my pace, slowly.
Anticipation of death is simply like looking for a new job.
Then suddenly on a Sunday,
talking recklessly while eating brunch,
a gristly piece of meat lodges in my throat.
I struggle for breath, too annoyed to be scared.
Someone pounds my back to no avail.
Out of nowhere, an alert pint-sized waiter
performs the Heimlich maneuver.
I don't believe it will work.
It does! Uncorked, I am freed.
Looking up I see the concerned visage and reversed collar
of a retired Navy chaplain,
pinch-hitting as God's messenger for the day.
Had he come to perform the last rites,
to ease my passage from this world to the hereafter?
Don't jump to dark conclusions.
In World War II on active duty,
he learned the Heimlich as well as the *himmlisch*.
Knowing it is best administered
to a standing victim,
he rushed to intervene.
On this day I am twice blessed
with the kindness of strangers.

A Poem with a Future Longing in It

The peach orchard off Rte. 57 is where
I wasn't this summer;
ditto Miiska's strawberry field.
Ben lets us pick over the rows
once the season tops its curve, and he
begins to have enough of stooping.
The berries plucked in their fat shine.

There are years unharvested,
everything ripe too fast, not put by.
Not exactly out of choice. Or
maybe choice slipped in as accident —
seed stuck on a bird's feet. Some years
you pick the peaches, and they rot
on the back porch in a day of hot weather.

In January catalogues bloom
delphiniums the color of long evenings.

And all this day has had a rustle in it
from these yellow and ochre leaves
staining the air. A restless falling.
The peaches we would have eaten
in February dark, their orange-yellow,
slippery, a little frozen
still in the middle, each slice red-fringed
where pit and flesh once joined.

Autumn Shrugs

Autumn shrugs—the salad greens are embittered
choose not to bolt to seed—shade to malachite
and verdigris instead of verdancy.

Wither instead of luscious rot in the compost heap
the collapse of the Cucurbita family—autumn
has broken them.

The Cabbage White has gone to ground—the worms
I dig seem somehow urgent as if they cannot bear
the air on their skin.

There is a new order to everything—long shadows
lie over us—prefiguring early spring, I embed
broad beans, one at a time.

They will overwinter stoically—among the parsnips
and kohlrabi—yes, they will taste of rusty nails
and set my teeth on edge. Come spring.

Eleanor Leonne Bennett, photograph

181

Old School

Like the octogenarian who warned me away
from his horse's back hooves —
He's still got a bit of dirt in him.

The horse a chestnut with a white eye rolling back,
a white snowball splash on one buttock.
The old man sat him as if a horse clapped

between his legs wasn't something he even had
to think about, his personal sense of distance
included how far a horse could shy

or tittup. He had looked bereft trudging across
the warm-up ring on only two of his legs,
he had been brought low

and didn't know why, puzzled by this pedestrian
way of travelling. Then he reached for the reins,
a man drawing a deep breath after

suffering, and up aloft stepping from the iron bangle
with one swift gesture. He kicked the green horse
into a rocking canter, saluting the judge,

a touch to his brim with the butt of his crop, and began
his round as he had always begun, pulling
the horse off the jump with one long rein,

then turning him onto it, the signal to take it. Once over,
again, opening his hand to steer him away.
They went clear, but in the jump-off

you are riding for time, so he can't win with this stately
tacking course, you won't see anyone else
these days riding like this.

They bounce their horses into the fence, release at take-off
for the bascule, the rising arch of the back,
and on landing gather up the impetus.

He is using an old-school technique, out of a museum,
we are watching the last of something, a bygone,
but it is still effective, in the long run.

Chico Seay, photograph

Recall

We're that couple standing at the edge.
Debt, second breakfast, a generous

shimmer over appalling depth.
Shore birds, sinking heels, sequences

beginning to fail. All day drowsiness
dogged me. We rose before five a.m.

Then—try to remember. Slowly,
a picture, a zigzag stairway up

from the beach and that's it.
Here, the banked cloud hovers

over the spray, the grass so young
it pokes up peacock blue

against the past, the brown past
dropping an empty crab, curling over.

This is the painful stamp of aging,
the picture beyond recall.

My mind, increasingly quiet, but who,
I reason, would fuss face out

to the shore with you, reading in a chair,
the cloth rim of your hat a tender

curve around everything, yes
I remember, the climb up sweet hillsides,

your body over mine and under, salt
cove behind your knee, a great

guffaw of foreplay. And just today
as we passed, the breeze picked up

a few shoots on the dune,
turquoise in the sun and silver.

Post Op

Looking down is all, the tangle
and tuft matting deep

in the berm. Our cuffs bristle
in seed and we make the shy

gestures of those who bruise
another's thoughts, pillow slip

apart down a muddy path. Blue
over the bluff, briefly an arc

of giant wings. Within her sleeve,
the scar rises still, its bumpy ridge

not really fading. Weeks of illness
scraped clear off the kitchen calendar.

Snow for a while, loud pellets,
nylon jackets, softening at last

to blanket the black dog.
Roots snake across the path,

gleaming in ice. Her fingers now
may practice again their forgotten

stretch. Each night we trail
something rough, something

smooth, over hyper-sensitive skin.
We gaze down and we count

out loud, how far, how steep
the path and curving.

Scribe

I don't know myself—that's all I know.
Where I am now is anyone's guess,
And yet the question of where to go
To find a solid landmark is less
Urgent than it was some years ago.

This is no slow, lazy decline
Into indifference. Rather
It's instinct, trying to refine
Beyond language. When the feather

Settles gently on the scale
My heart will float easily,
Without a word . . . or else fail.

For a frozen moment
I remain dead silent

On the hard museum floor.
Two browsers glance lazily
At a stone figure before

Drifting away and leaving me
With this gem of antiquity.
The trusting eyes forever see
Up the ray of eternity

Toward a verdict not yet declared.
Patience. For millennia this scribe's
Unwavering attention has dared
To wait unanswered. His face describes
What it means to be truly prepared.

The balance of the poem reflects the perfect balance of the
Egyptian weighing of the heart against a feather.

Poems

They hover on the outskirts of our lives
like mosquitoes,
their voices as grudgingly welcome
as the calls of crows
scrubbing across snow.

We forgive them their trespasses
as one forgives a toddler tugging a sleeve,
but they intrude
in the way that a woman
smashes the six settings
of her mother's antique Spode
at a garden party, beside the white verbena.

Eleanor Leonne Bennett, photograph

Water Lilies in Evening

after Monet, 1916-1922

How calm when night
comes on and reflections
disappear, and duties
of work subside.

Time to go inside
and wash up.
The lilies have closed
and disappeared.

Leave it to the crickets,
frogs, the owl
who wakes you.
You, too, will fold
in darkness, dream
you're trying to grasp
stems rooted in water—
yellow green gray
murky brown.

Tomorrow will bring
the light, and you'll
begin again, and through
the long and short days of the years
marked with candles, sorrow,
the hungry birds return.
Watch them on branches—
the masked cardinal,
the blue jay thief,
the curious wren
who sings and sings.

The Commission

Artist: What shall populate this still life?

We bought pears of burnished bronze and yellow
with a red glow, apples green and blood red, an orange,
kumquats with fresh greens attached, a pomegranate.

And as he arranged our fruit on white Italian ceramic
we walked about the house plucking out objects
to fill the allotted space—woven raffia from the Congo,

a Dogon mask, a leatherbound volume from Florence—
all arranged and rearranged, some discarded,
while we added a glass blue-cobalt pitcher,

a florid Deruta candlestick, substituted a tablecloth
of green damask and one of white embroidery.
He draped the cloths, sculptural ridges and folds

embraced the selected forms. We added our gold-framed
wedding portrait, placed it next to the ceramic bowl
and in front of the candlestick. Kumquats overflowed

a dish resting on Florentine leather.
The blue-cobalt pitcher held two white lilies
resting against white. We watched as brush strokes

transformed the narrative of our lives heavy with objects,
as he focused on the whiteness of the lilies repeated
against the whiteness of the white embroidered cloth.

Muthwa's Infusions

Muthwa roams through the grassy slopes,
examines carefully each pea-like bloom.
The ones chosen are cut gently
from their stems and fill her basket.
In spring and summer *Sutherlandia's*
red-purple mosaics these dry grasslands.
The San call the flower *insisa*, the one
who dispels darkness; *unwele* whispers
the Zulu *sangomas; kankerbossie,*
cancer bush, the Afrikaners name it.
At the clinic door in dusty Kraafontein,
the depressed and arthritic, the ulcerous
and asthmatic, the cancerous and those
whom Cape Town doctors send home to die
wait for Muthwa. They wait for infusions
of *Sutherlandia's* flowers to drink or to cover
their ravaged flesh and eat the mush
of millet grain as Muthwa invokes ancestors'
names. Last month an old woman
was brought on a pallet, today she walks home.
Now researchers scour the Western Cape
to harvest *Sutherlandia,* its flowers transmuted
to tablets and gels. But in dusty Kraafontein
those the Cape Town doctors send home
to die still wait at the clinic door for Muthwa's
infusions, millet mush, and incantations.

Still Life with Occupational Hazards

I have killed rats
in their lairs under listing sheds,
and have tracked unrepentant termites
through the dark crumble
of masticated rot.

In my time I have knelt
over a forest of lumber,
my hammer sounding the framer's prayer.
And I have slunk along the ridgelines
of teetering roofs on thankless tasks.

I've left blood on the job
by the hour and by the piece,
and have fought off exhaustion,
spasm and rage. Like so many of us,
I learn the hard way.

There are always occupational hazards,
and strands of decision to splice.

Saw axe sledge blade
hunger family child.

Gertrude: The Stein Collection

If he asked me if I liked it
If I told him would he like it. *
Would he like it if I told him
the wheelchair was in the way?

Fine for my long-standing husband,
but I was pushing the chair,
suffering complaints about my driving,
warnings of near-missed ankles or shins,
and navigating for a frontrow seat
before Picasso or Matisse
proved major distractions —

until we came to Gertrude
settled Buddha-like on a pedestal,
relaxed in the folds and creases
of her fully rounded bronze girth,
one shirt button left undone,
hands resting on a skirt pulled taut
across parted knees. Hair pulled back in a bun,
light reflecting from cheekbones and chin.

Leaning forward
as if she had something to confide
inviting the viewer to linger, come closer
caught in her gaze and sheer presence.

There was there there.

*"If I Told Him. A Completed Portrait of Picasso,"
Gertrude Stein, 1923

New Hat

Say it's the undercurrent.
You come back from the undercurrent, one foot still
in the undercurrent. And what kind of person
has a desire like that? There's nothing but outside forces,

unfittable pages, perplexed pages, all the pages until empty
of pages. Optimism. Insufficiently. Impractically.
The stasis of excess is enough. The exhilaration of incompleteness:
once. The misrule of chance convinces, connivance

or not. The worship of pages is endless. I need a new hat,
man, I need a different head. I'll take another one, this time
with a harder brim to withstand the undercurrent.
If there were someone in there other than him what else would

I inquire about? What else would he remember or concede
that hasn't already been unthreaded, or stifled?
The worship of sex is endless. Every matinee. Remember them?
I read the permanent monogamous version again. The title to the song

in my head: "I think I would like to." Maybe it was a random phrase
I mistook for a song. There was no melody. All the follow-up tunes
have the same Innuendo: The Pillow Book of twenty-four years,
The Kama Sutra after middle age. The ongoing, unpredictably,
irregularly. Right after dinner.

Say it's the undercurrent and say it
doesn't always elevate—and it does—and it discontinues—and
refortifies—and revertifies. The longer it all goes the more indeterminate,
the less indefinite it is predicting the face you look at in your head. It really is

that vague. It really is that precise. Just a second, just a second,
I saw my hair as a boy, the people around me spoke with assurance
and affection. We rowed into the lake, I wanted the duck on my knee.
Unsatisfied rapture. From my bench the hibiscus blossoms looked so pale
watermelon red they appeared like a formation of powder, almost

blurry. A breeze increased the effect of the pallor. I could hear the rock band Slave Behave, which meant the opposite. There was no melody, there was something else, it was another dialect, there was a kind of breath, it came from the direction of The Tower of the Winds, it had sprawl, there was no rim,

the tempo kept rising and trailing off, it seemed from one of the cats picking over the food wrappings, half of the copper sun left the columns, it made me shift, you get a pressure, you get a craving, it sings itself raw inside of you.

Title to the Pump

That remote village in southern Crete
where the bus with most of its paint
worn off blew out a back tire.

That twelve-foot Vigeland* realism
bronze sculpture village man and boy
walking hands held monument

in the village square. Commemorated
complete rounding-up of males ages
ten to sixty, world war the second,

twentieth century grave dump village.
The passenger who'd been sleeping
under an archeological map told me

the statue plaque inscription story,
shot down into the self-dug hole,
the labor-saving act right to the end.

The last century outstanding at the
self-dug hole, it was a self-dug labor-
extracting pump. No reason to think

---

*Norwegian sculptor Gustav Vigeland was noted for his
massive figurative sculpture.

anybody'll stop having the need.
The shrewdly accomplished global land
management population labor livestock

water supply management need. Is that it?
The re-expressed need in Afghanistan, Iraq,
Palestine and the upcoming places, unless

the other terrorists get there first. For the
need. Confucius wrote down on a leaf with
a ragged surface, "Within the four seas

all men are brothers." Maybe it was a
split surface. The footnote at the bottom
of the leaf was erased in my edition. Started

with this day because one of ours was the
Desert Storm Shock and Awe Paymaster
General, and finished reading on this exact

day loaned copies of *The Uses and Abuses
of Argument, The Little Brown Reader, The
Practical Guide to Writing* a neighbor teacher

gave me, but you never saw in a single
square foot of built-in kitchenette table space
so much useless junk-language in your life

to get through this life — the uses and abuses,
the little brown, the storm, a practical guide,
loose bowels, loosing bowels is more like it,

a lifetime policy, the Vet's wife and
sister lifting the prosthetic husband
into his chair, every desert they can

make, every emotion in the book, the reason
I started, every appeal, the reason at all.

Post Laryngoscopy, I Follow News
of the Trapped Miners

Passages collapse. Some take decades to fail. Seven
miles of tunnel one man ran daily, then sang,
shirtless, sulfurous, *Love me tender.* I was ice-

packed, feared nails had shut my airways.
Each man entered a tube and was taken up:
thirty-three lives predicted, *Never again normal.*

Fluttering in my ear as if a dozen bats wanted out.
The miners were blindfolded against brilliance.

I felt the collar that checks a dog's lurch.
Sutureless, I dreamt, *Larynx insouciant,* stamped to my report.
The tallest buildings are lower than the depths these men fed
against.

What had been *encrypted* was lifted from my *vallecula*:
there is a dock between *epiglottis* and tongue.
We learn words as we need them—emergent,

they scratched their names. Men of the fist to the table,
daughter swung and set down gently. My inconvenience
was not cancer but, *put under,*

a soul worries. A swallow winged up grit and my diction
shattered. We choose to sing or cringe in pain's company.
We rest on whom we never knew as the beloved.

Yet, quickly, we lose the tenderness fear gave us, the bell to ask,
back on the shelf. I wanted to see what the scope saw.
The miners wanted to get laid, then drink alone.

I should have stayed breakable. We learn
new words and then forget them.

Red

Not your careless footfall in the tall grass
of the old apple orchard
that spooked the red-tail from her perch
in the low height of the dead elm,
but the light rattle of the dried seed pods
on the cow vetch tangled around your ankle,
shaking softly with each step—
that tender alarm, the pepper of surprise.
And she screeched her annoyance at you
as she took off across the valley,
spreading wide the redness of that tail
so you would know to name her.

Robins in Elmwood

The robin drop-dives from the top of the old willow,
skims the surface of the grass, swoops up sharp and smooth
then lights upon the tip of an obelisk, perches there,
sure-footed, steady as the stone itself, then moves like breath
to Farrand's grave. Another sits on Lothrop's stone, another
on McGraw's, and there on Whitney's "Perpetual Care,"
on Pennycook, on Kahn.

They never stumble to the perch, but like attracting force,
like light, they hit and sit, then wait for me to pass.
Am I some small caravan to notice for the seconds it takes
for me to disappear; or do they share this curiosity —
as I enjoy their grace perhaps they like to stop and watch
the clumsy pattern of my step, the way my eyes turn
to their movement; am I part of their game?

They like the openness of sepulchers, monuments, corners
exposed, stone trunks, crosses, the head of any statue there,
the headless statue too. Their gray backs on the grayness of stone,
their breasts a setting sun, an open wound, a measure of the life
that lifts them up and off again to willows, the high green canopy
of oak and ash, white pine and sycamore.

Dancing with Grandma

*In Madagascar many Christians and practitioners
of traditional ancestor worship participate in death-
dancing by pulling the remains of loved ones from the
tomb, dancing with the corpses, then carefully rewrapping
them for re-interment.*
— Milwaukee Journal Sentinel

I wrap you in blue wool
like the sweater you wore
when I thought
you looked like sky,
tie seven knots to hold you
and dance with your bones
before the weather warms.
I tell you of Grandpa,
how he died in his sleep
and was found still warm
under the electric blanket
like the bread dough you covered
with a towel in your gas oven.
I say Maraleen moved
to New Mexico near Corinne
and her Navajo husband;
and Glenn fell off a roof,
smashed his ankle
just before Thanksgiving.

But maybe you know these things
and watch me play the record
I gave you and listen
to Tennessee Ernie Ford.
We waltz on your grave,
sway and turn, then return you
to rest with instant coffee
in a china cup and a sugar cookie
on a flowered plate from your kitchen
which still smells of pickled apples,
strawberries and molasses.

On Turning Fifty-five

When I was eighteen,
my biology teacher took me to the zoo
during spring break
to see the koalas mate,
which made my friends envious,
and their jealousy was justified
since we all thought she loved me.

Miss _____ and I stood
by the cage eating Cracker Jacks
while one male scent marked
his prowess and bellowed.
She grabbed my hand and explained
how the loops, whorls, and arches
of koala fingerprints resembled ours
more than they resembled chimpanzees'.

I told her chickens loved the faces
of pretty girls, so on our way home,
we ate at Koo Koo Roo's and pretended
our salads were eucalyptus.
Then we bellowed across the parking lot
sharing the last drumstick.

And that was all I told my friends,
since even then I knew that primates
of the higher order never kiss and tell.
But last night when I saw her on TV,
playing "Name That Tune"
with rhesus monkeys, and one recognized
"Old MacDonald" before she did,

I wondered if maybe true love
would have made a difference;
you know, if I had shared
a young woman's aging,
an old woman's changing,
the guilt of pleasure bellowing?

On Not Knowing

When I was young, I watched
a Chinese monk brush characters
of red lacquer on a door
the color of spoiled plums;
no matter what his message,
I felt the impatience of not knowing,
and something changed in my heart.

And here lies the struggle,
the uncertainty in wondering
if there is anything
more certain than losing my hat
when I leaned into sunset
sighting a humpback whale,
the weight of its bones
bearing hard to lee,
stunning in aptitude and joy;
its molecules speaking a language
I did not understand.

Aspirations

*It is almost unbelievable that the insects should have undergone
several stages of metamorphosis within the sinuses.*
—from "Myasis Resulting from the Use of the
Aspirator Method In the Collection of Insects"
by Paul D. Hurd, Jr., *Science*, June 1954

Summer, 1953.
Paul D. Hurd, Jr., is in Point Barrow, Alaska,
collecting bees with an aspirator, a device
consisting of a stoppered vial, two copper tubes,
a rubber tube, a fine mesh brass screen and two lips (his),
unaware that, a few months from now,
three adult rove beetles, thirteen fungus gnat larvae,
three egg parasite wasps and fifty springtails
will crawl, ooze, fly and spring from his nose
and make their new home in California.

This is how life works. You go to Alaska to collect bees,
and you wind up with adult rove beetles in California.
Or in the case of the painter, Samuel F. B. Morse,
you go to Paris with aspirations of becoming America's Rembrandt,
spending two years in the gallery of the Louvre
painting (what else?) *The Gallery of the Louvre*,
until one day you take a walk outside Paris
and notice flag-waving Frenchmen atop wooden towers,
and you wind up in New York inventing the telegraph.

Or you're me, and you spend the late 1970's
aspiring to qualify for the 1980 Olympic Marathon Trials—
as likely as a fungus gnat larva metamorphosing into a parasite wasp—
when you find yourself somewhere over the Caribbean
in a Cessna Golden Eagle with Elliott, your rich, octogenarian pilot
who has organized *The First International Saint Kitts Half Marathon*,
"*international*" meaning a few guys from Nevis, two or three from Trinidad,
three hundred or so Kittitians
and the five of you from Elliott's home town in Indiana
on your way to race a lap around the island,

your plane a tiny, smooth-gliding silhouette
on the aquamarine waters below
until you suddenly lose what seems a thousand feet
in the time it takes Elliott to turn toward you and yell,

GRAB SOME LUGGAGE TO EJECT!
WE'RE GOING DOWN!

❊

In his 1974 classic, *Zen and the Art of Motorcycle Maintenance*,
Robert Pirsig writes,

> You look at where you're going and where you are
> and it never makes sense, but then you look back
> *at where you've been and a pattern seems to emerge.*

And though I would not call it a particularly clear pattern,
I can make out a line weaving through a second career,
a new house, a wedding, a first career and there,
somewhere between Fort Lauderdale and Puerto Rico,
a falling Cessna Golden Eagle with me stuffing my copy
of *Zen and the Art of Motorcycle Maintenance* into my red backpack
as Elliott's laughter dawns on me like a Caribbean sunrise.

But here in an adult rove beetle stage—and then some—
life makes as much sense as sucking bees in a Point Barrow meadow
or sitting in the gallery of the Louvre painting thirty-eight teeny replicas
of the masterworks around you on one canvas. Then again,
it's more like *walking* beneath fierce equatorial sunlight
through the 10-mile mark of a 13-mile footrace
just before a kind Saint Kitts woman offers you a cup of water
and you stop to take a sip and then
                              a breath.

Against Nostalgia

Because I suspect that it is nostalgia, and I suspect that nostalgia
    is love of the self masquerading as love of the world,
        I have tried not to speak of the Woolworth's five-and-dime

at the corner of Court Street and Water. I have tried not to show
    that I remember, enjoy remembering, running my hand
        along the scalloped edge of the bolts of fabric, while the smell

of hot popcorn, at first sickening, grew distant, then delicious.
    I have tried not to admit that I savor the buttery air of Woolworth's
        as others savor the salt and brine of a youthful trip to Calais,

my Calais, circa 1965, Binghamton, New York, where almost
    anyone who had been to France had been there as a soldier.
        Veterans of The Great War, we still called it that, sat

at the Formica lunch counter, drinking coffee, cigarette balanced on the edge
    of the saucer as wide dull-bladed fans spun overhead.
        Because I suspect that nostalgia is love of love itself, unencumbered

by effort or consequence, uncomplicated by responsibility or fear,
    I have tried not to wander those aisles, no one thing more important
        than another, not the white anklet nor the hairnet,

not the doily nor the handsaw, nor the display where the bicycle
    and the sled stood side by side, as if there were no seasons, or all
        seasons were one. I have denied my love for the parakeets

that sang in their cages, except for the day when someone unlatched the little doors
    and the birds, like turquoise and tangerine cellophane, flew under the fans,
        over the two glass vats of lemonade, pink and pale green, ceaselessl

tumbling through themselves. Employees with butterfly nets ran that day
    through Woolworth's, where I first learned that one thing
        can be exchanged for another: a quarter for a card of shirt buttons

or a box of eight crayons, a dollar for a metal picture frame, for a rain bonnet
that, in theory, would fit back into its hinge-topped plastic capsule,
which I loved, that small compartment impervious to rain.

Because I suspect that nostalgia may be love of the best self, that small part
that is giving and forgiving, that nostalgia at best may be practice
for loving the present, I indulge myself in remembering

the lunch counter's red vinyl stools, reserved for the veterans, who sat
shoulder to shoulder, talking about sports and the weather,
who sometimes just nodded and reached

into a shirt-pocket for a pack of Lucky Strikes, tapped one out,
offered it, lit it with a flick of the wrist. I remember the economy
of the gesture, the brief flame, the ribbon of smoke,

although I suspect that I do not remember, rather, imagine,
as I imagine that one man carried a bullet beneath a rib,
and another man carried a rabbit's foot spotted with blood.

Because I suspect that nostalgia may be the desire to exchange one's life
for another life, or to exchange one version of one's life
for another version, in which one lived more deeply,

I come down hard against nostalgia, as my chest slammed
onto the Flexible Flier which, in truth, I never enjoyed
except for the part where I was indoors, and warm again.

be granite

stolid   immovable
impervious to flame
or rising river   to straight-line winds
glittering gold by day   burnished silver
under the hunger moon

blind

let glaciers crash into the ocean
& monsoons fail
let wheat & maize
shrink   rice shrivel
mountain snows disappear

let each footfall raise dust
be silent
be stone

From the collection of the Managing Editor, photograph

In the Fullness

I am created over and again
by every lightspill under thunderclouds
and by the clouds themselves sighing
on the river, by every explosion
of eagle from the ancient white pine
and by the pine itself which shushes
the wind's complaint.

O the bullfrog drums in his throat
and wolves' voices bell
against the darkening moon. My blood howls.
Ganglia, epidermis, organs, bones
remember. There
was the beginning, and here,
here it comes again.

DIANA ANHALT is the author of *A Gathering of Fugitives* (Archer Books), a chapbook, *Shiny Objects*, and essays, articles, and book reviews in both English and Spanish. Her second chapbook, *Second Skin*, was recently released. Her poems have appeared in *Nimrod*, *Atlanta Review*, *The Sow's Ear Poetry Review*, and *BorderSenses*, among other journals.

SUZE BARON was born in Port-au-Prince, Haiti, and now lives in Brooklyn, New York. She is a retired Registered Nurse and a family tree enthusiast, who writes poetry and prose in Haitian Creole and in English. She has published in *The New York Quarterly*, *The International Women's Writing Guild Network*, *Spillway*, *Nimrod*, *Z-Miscellaneous*, *Le Matin*, and elsewhere.

DANIEL BECKER practices and teaches internal medicine at the University of Virginia School of Medicine in Charlottesville, Virginia. The fact that 2013 is the Year of the Snake had nothing to do with making this poem, "Serpentarium," but he feels it is an interesting coincidence.

DIANE BURTON, Associate Editor of *Nimrod*, teaches writing and literature at The University of Tulsa.

JUDITH CHALMER's most recent publications include a second book of haiku and tanka translations, *Deepening Snow*, with author Michiko Oishi (Plowboy Press 2012), first prize in the Newberger Poetry Contest of *Lilith Magazine*, and publication of two poems in the Spring 2012 issue of *The DMQ Review*. She is Director of VSA Vermont, a nonprofit organization devoted to arts and disabilities.

ROBIN CHAPMAN's most recent book is *One Hundred White Pelicans* (Tebot Bach 2013). She is the recipient of *Appalachia*'s 2010 Poetry Prize and a Wisconsin Arts Board Literary Arts Fellowship. Her poems have appeared recently in *Alaska Quarterly Review*, *Prairie Schooner*, *qarrtsiluni*, *Valparaiso Poetry Review*, and *Wilderness House Literary Review*.

OLEG CHUKHONSEV is a contemporary Russian poet. His awards include the State Prize of the Russian Federation for Literature, The State Pushkin Prize, The Boris Pasternak Award, and the Russian National Prize "The Poet," among others.

JOANNE M. CLARKSON is the author of two poetry collections, *Pacing the Moon* (Chantry Press) and *Crossing without Daughters* (March Street Press). Her work appears regularly in small-press publications, including *Valparaiso Poetry Review*, *Paterson Literary Review*, and *Amoskeag*. She has a Master's Degree in English; she currently works as Registered Nurse specializing in Hospice and Community Nursing.

SUZANNE CLEARY was the 2011 2nd Prize winner of *Nimrod*'s Poetry Prize, and she won the 2012 John Ciardi Prize for Poetry for her manuscript *Beauty Mark,* to be published in 2013 by BkMk Press, of the University of Missouri-Kansas City. Her previous books are *Keeping Time* and *Trick Pear.* Professor of English at SUNY Rockland, she also teaches in the low-residency M.F.A. program of Converse College.

JENNIFER COMPTON was born in New Zealand and now lives in Melbourne, Australia. *This City* won the Kathleen Grattan Award in New Zealand and was published by Otago University Press in 2011. *Barefoot* (Picaro Press) was short-listed for the John Bray Award in 2012, and *Ungainly* has recently been published by Mulla Mulla Press.

LORNA CROZIER lives on Vancouver Island, where she is a Distinguished Professor at the University of Victoria. She has won Canada's top poetry prize, the Governor-General's Literary Award. Her latest book of poetry is *The Book of Marvels: A Compendium of Everyday Things.*

IVY DEMPSEY has published poems in *Southern Poetry Review, Chariton Review,* CALYX, and other journals. *The Scent of Water: New & Selected Poems* won the 2002 Oklahoma Book Award, and the *Midwest Quarterly: 100 Poems from 50 Years* included her poem "Beyond Doors."

STEPHEN DUNN is the author of 17 books of poems, including *Different Hours,* which was awarded the Pulitzer Prize. His next collection, *Lines of Defense,* will be published by W. W. Norton and Company at the end of 2013. He lives in Frostburg, Maryland, and is Distinguished Professor at Richard Stockton College.

SUSAN EISENBERG is a Resident Artist/Scholar at Brandeis University's Women's Studies Research Center. She is author of *Blind Spot,* a poetry collection; *We'll Call You If We Need You,* a non-fiction work; and *Perpetual Care,* a forthcoming collection of poetry and photography. Her mixed media art installation, *On Equal Terms,* exhibits fall 2013 at the Clemente Soto Velez Center in New York City.

CHARLES ENTREKIN's works include the novel, *Red Mountain, Birmingham, Alabama, 1965,* and *Listening: New and Selected Works.* He was a founder and editor of *Berkeley Poets Cooperative* and *The Berkeley Poets Workshop & Press,* co-founder of Literature Alive!, co-editor of the e-zine *Sisyphus,* and managing editor of *Hip Pocket Press.*

JEAN ESTEVE, painter and poet, lives on the Oregon coast. Her third chapbook, *Off-Key,* was a 2013 finalist for the Oregon Book Award in poetry. A full collection, *The Winter Sun*, is due out this year from Turn-stone Books of Oregon.

LAUREL FEIGENBAUM credits the University of California, Berkeley, and Wordsworth for her love of poetry. It was not until after family and careers in education and business that she gathered late-life courage and began writing, finding the world around her a constant source of inspiration. She lives with her husband of sixty-three years just north of San Francisco.

DAVID LEE GARRISON's poems have appeared in *Barrow Street*, *Connecticut Review*, *Rattle*, and other journals; they have also been read on *The Writer's Almanac* by Garrison Keillor and featured by Ted Kooser on his website, American Life in Poetry. His new book is *Playing Bach in the D. C. Metro* (Browser Books, 2012).

ROBERT GETHNER is a Professor of Mathematics at Franklin & Marshall College in Lancaster, Pennsylvania. His poems have previously appeared in *The Madison Review*, *The Midwest Quarterly*, *Connecticut River Review*, *Hawai'i Pacific Review*, *Mathematics Magazine*, *The Journal of the American Medical Association*, and *Blue Unicorn*.

BRITTON GILDERSLEEVE, former director of the Oklahoma State University Writing Project, serves on the Board of Trustees for the Oklahoma Humanities Council. She spent her childhood in Asia and several years in the Middle East. Her work has appeared in *New Millennium Writings*, *Passager*, *Atlas Poetica*, and other journals. She has written three chapbooks.

JEFF GUNDY's sixth book of poems, *Somewhere Near Defiance*, is forthcoming from Anhinga Press. Other new poems are in *The Sun*, *The Cincinnati Review*, *Kenyon Review*, *The Hamilton Stone Review*, and *The Christian Century*. An essay based on his 2008 Fulbright lectureship at the University of Salzburg is forthcoming in *The Georgia Review*. He teaches English at Bluffton University in Ohio.

CYNTHIA GUSTAVSON is a psychotherapist and leader in the field of poetry therapy. She is the author of *In-Versing Your Life* (2006), *Bully! The Big Book for Bullies and the Bullied*, and has won awards for her children's book *Ballad of the Rag Man* and her poetry collection *Please Use This for Children and Not for War and Guns*. She lives in Tulsa, Oklahoma.

MEREDITH DAVIES HADAWAY is the author of two poetry collections, *The River is a Reason* (2011) and *Fishing Secrets of the Dead* (2005). In addition to publishing poems and reviews in various literary journals, she serves as poetry editor for *The Summerset Review*. She is Vice President of College Relations and Marketing for Washington College.

JOHN HARRIS's poems have appeared in various journals. He lives in Savannah, Georgia.

HARRY HUMES's first poetry collection, *Winter Weeds*, received the Devins Award for Poetry. His most recent collections are *Butterfly Effect*, a National Poetry Series selection, and *August Evening With Trumpet*. Poems of his have been published in *Poetry Northwest*, *The Gettysburg Review*, *Shenandoah*, *Hampden-Sydney Poetry Review*, *The Hollins Critic* and elsewhere.

DEBORAH J. HUNTER is a poet, spoken-word artist, actor, and workshop facilitator. Her poetry has appeared in both literary journals and anthologies. She received the Jingle Feldman Artist Award in 2000 and was nominated for Oklahoma Poet Laureate in 2012. Her spoken-word performance pieces include *Amazons, Gypsies and Wandering Minstrels*, and *Bayou Stories*.

JEFFREY JOHANNES is a poet/artist whose work has appeared in *Rosebud*, *Graphic Classics*, *Modern Haiku*, and *English Journal*. He won the 2012 Hal Grutzmacher Poetry Award, sponsored by *Peninsula Pulse*. His latest projects are cartoons of his poems, which he calls "pometoons," and finishing his first collection of poetry, *Ritual for Beginning Again*. He lives in Port Edwards, Wisconsin.

DANIELLE JONES has a Ph.D. in poetry from SUNY-Albany and an M.F.A. in creative nonfiction from Seattle Pacific University. She teaches literature and writing at the Univerity of Montana Western.

ALLAN KAPLAN is a retired teacher. He has published two books, *Paper Airplane* (Harper & Row), and *Like One of Us* (Untitled). His work has been published in a variety of journals, including *The Paris Review*, *Slant Magazine*, *The Iowa Review*, *Green Hills Literary Lantern*, and *Chiron Review*.

BECKY KENNEDY is a linguist and college professor who lives with her family in Jamaica Plain, Massachusetts. Her poetry has appeared in many magazines and journals, as well as a chapbook published by Finishing Line Press. Her work has been nominated for a Pushcart Prize and has appeared on *Verse Daily*.

TED KOOSER served two terms as U. S. Poet Laureate, and during his second term was awarded the Pulitzer Prize in Poetry for one of his twelve books of poety, *Delights and Shadows*. His two most recent books are for children, and a third is on the way. He lives in rural Nebraska.

211

SUSANNE KORT is a psychotherapist practicing in Jalisco, Mexico. In the U.S., her poetry has appeared in the *The North American Review*, *Notre Dame Review*, *Grand Street*, *Green Mountains Review*, *Indiana Review*, *Seneca Review*, *Prairie Schooner*, *Sonora Review*, *The Laurel Review*, and other journals. Her work has also been published in journals in Ireland, England, and Canada.

MICHAEL LAUCHLAN's poems have appeared in many publications including *New England Review*, *The Virginia Quarterly Review*, *The North American Review*, *The Innisfree Poetry Journal*, *Crab Creek Review*, and *The Cortland Review*, and have been included in two anthologies, *Abandon Automobile* from WSU Press and *A Mind Apart* from Oxford. He has been awarded the Consequence Prize in Poetry.

SUSANNAH LAWRENCE is the author of two books on natural history and has worked as a consumer activist, environmental lobbyist, and freelance writer, though not all at the same time. She recently received her M.F.A. in poetry from the Vermont College of Fine Arts. She lives in Norfolk, Connecticut.

LORI LEVY has lived in Vermont, Israel, and Los Angeles. Her poems have appeared in *Poet Lore*, *Rattle*, *The MacGuffin*, *The Comstock Review*, and a variety of other literary journals in the U.S., as well as journals in England and Israel. Her health-related poems have appeared in medical and health journals in the U.S.

SANDY LONGLEY is an Associate Professor of Literature at Columbia-Greene Community College in New York's Hudson River Valley. She has recently been published in *Spillway*, *Southword*, *The Naugatuck River Review*, and *Down in the Dirt*. Her poems have been short-listed for the U.K.'s Bridport Prize, Ireland's *Fish Anthology*, and *Atlanta Review's* International Prize.

PERIE LONGO, Poet Laureate *Emerita* of Santa Barbara, California, has authored three volumes of poetry, the latest titled *With Nothing behind but Sky: a journey through grief*. A forthcoming book is slated for January, 2014. Recipient of three Pushcart nominations, she has published poems in many journals and anthologies including *Atlanta Review*, *International Poetry Review*, *Nimrod*, *Paterson Literary Review*, and *Prairie Schooner.*

B. D. LOVE, the American name of the Chinese poet Lan Yan, is both a novelist and a poet. He has published three novels: *DragonBlossom* under his American name; *A Day in the Life of a Severed Head*, and *Song of the Ten Thousands* under his Chinese name. The poem published in this issue of

Nimrod is part of a large sequence involving existential curiosities through the prism of dog ownership.

MARGARET MACKINNON's work has appeared in various journals, including *Poetry, New England Review, The Georgia Review,* and *Valparaiso Poetry Review*. She won the Richard Eberhart Poetry Prize from Florida State University and the Graybeal-Gowen Poetry Prize from *Shenandoah*. Her book of poems, *The Invented Child*, will be published in 2013.

RITA MARIA MAGDALENO was born in Augsburg, Germany. Her poetic memoir, *Marlene Dietrich, Rita Hayworth, & My Mother*, was published by University of Arizona Press. She teaches memoir, journal writing and poetry in Arizona schools. She is a Registered Nurse and facilitates "Writing & Healing" workshops. She lives in Tucson.

MARY MCCARTHY is a retired teacher and social worker who lives and writes in Berkeley, California. Her poems have appeared in *Blue Unicorn, California Quarterly, Milvia Street Art and Literary Journal, Ruah: A Journal of Spiritual Poetry,* an anthology, *Through Corridors of Light,* and other publications.

JO MCDOUGALL lives in Leawood, Kansas. She is the author of five books of poetry, the most recent being *Satisfied With Havoc* (Autumn House Press). Her chapbook, *Under an Arkansas Sky*, was published in 2010 (Tavern Books) and her memoir, *Daddy's Money: a Memoir of Farm and Family*, was published in 2011 (University of Arkansas Press).

CLAUDIA MONPERE's poems and short stories have appeared in *Kenyon Review, Prairie Schooner, Spoon River Poetry Review, Puerto del Sol, Ecotone,* and elsewhere. She is a recipient of the *Georgetown Review* Fiction Award and teaches writing at Santa Clara University.

MARY JO MOORE has been writing poetry since the mid-1980s when she signed into a Writing Conference as a prose writer, but found the poetry workshops far more interesting. She currently teaches English as a Second Language to adults from all over the world.

CAROLINA MORALES is the author of three chapbooks of poetry, *Bride of Frankenstein and other poems, In Nancy Drew's Shadow,* and *Dear Monster,* all published by Finishing Line Press. Her poems have been nominated for three Pushcart prizes and have appeared in *Spoon River Poetry Review, Poet Lore, Paterson Literary Review, Journal of New Jersey Poets* and other journals.

HENRY MORGENTHAU, now ninety-six years old, was a television producer and writer. Based at Boston's station WGBH, his programs include the "Eleanor Roosevelt: Prospects of Mankind" series and the award-winning "South African Essay." His non-fiction writings include *Mostly Morgenthaus: A Family History*. Poetry is a delayed vocation. Thes two poems in this issue of *Nimrod* are his first submitted for publication.

CJ MUCHHALA's poems have appeared in anthologies, print, and on-line publications, in art and poetry installations, and on CD-ROM and audio CD. Her work has been nominated for the Best of the Net award and twice for the Pushcart Prize. She lives in Shorewood, Wisconsin.

ROBERTA MURPHY's earlier work has appeared twice in *Nimrod*, and also in *The Georgia Review, Other Voices, Harvard Review, The Laurel Review, Feminist Studies, The William and Mary Review*, and other magazines. She is the recipient of an NEA Fellowship for Creative Writers.

HELEN BETH O'NEAL lives in Tulsa, Oklahoma. She is an early childhood educator whose classroom curriculum revolves around nature. Her family enjoys hiking and she spends many hours tending her garden trying to create a happy balance using both ornamental and native plants. She would rather sit in a tree than an easy chair.

GAIL PECK is the author of three poetry chapbooks and three full-length collections, most recently *Counting the Lost*. Her poems and essays have appeared in numerous journals and anthologies including *The Southern Review, Nimrod, The Greensboro Review, Mississippi Review, Rattle*, and *Connotation Press*. Her work is forthcoming in *Alimentum*.

ORICK PETERSON telecommutes to her copywriting and editing job in Illinois from her home in Northfield, Minnesota. As the years pass, memory becomes a more and more compelling muse. Yet most of her poems now arise from the challenge of bringing to bear on present experiences the full complexity of seven decades of more-or-less conscious living.

ZARA RAAB has written two books, *Swimming the Eel* and *The Book of Gretel*. Her new book, *Rumpelstiltskin, or What's in a Name?*, will be published in 2013. She is a contributing editor to *Poetry Flash*. Her poems, reviews, and essays have appeared in *Arts & Letters, West Branch, The Evansville Review, River Styx, The Redwood Coast Review, The Dark Horse*, and elsewhere.

TOM RAITHEL retired six years ago from a thirty-year career in journalism. He grew up in Milwaukee, Wisconsin, and today lives with his wife, Theresa, and two dogs in Evansville, Indiana. His poems have appeared in *The Southern Review*, *The Midwest Quarterly*, *Atlanta Review*, *Poetry East*, and *Southern Poetry Review*.

DOUG RAMSPECK is the author of four poetry collections. His most recent book, *Mechanical Fireflies* (2011), received the Barrow Street Press Poetry Prize. His first book, *Black Tupelo Country* (2008), received the John Ciardi Prize for Poetry. His poems have appeared in journals that include *Slate*, *Kenyon Review*, *The Southern Review*, and *The Georgia Review*.

MARILYNN RASHID is a lecturer in Spanish at Wayne State University in Detroit, Michigan. Her poems have appeared in a number of publications, including *The Comstock Review*, *Black Dirt*, *The MacGuffin*, and *RUNES*. Her poetry translations have appeared in *Nimrod*, *The Marlboro Review*, *River Styx*, *Paintbrush: A Journal of Poetry & Translation*, and *Absinthe*.

JAMES REISS's latest book is *Riff on Six: New and Selected Poems*. His work has appeared in *The Atlantic Monthly*, *Esquire*, *The Nation*, *The New Republic Magazine*, *The New Yorker*, *The Paris Review*, *Poetry*, and *Slate*. After more than four decades of teaching and book editing at Miami University, he now lives with his wife near Chicago.

FRANCINE RINGOLD, Editor-in-Chief of *Nimrod* for over forty years, completed two terms as Oklahoma's Poet Laureate (2003-2005, 2005-2007). Her most recent book of poems, *Still Dancing*, won the Oklahoma Book Award in 2005. Her books include *The Trouble with Voices: Poetry*, another Oklahoma Book Award winner; and *Making Your Own Mark: Writing and Drawing for Senior Citizens*. Her newest book, *How Not to Write a Memoir*, and another volume of poetry *A Dog's Life*, are forthcoming in 2013.

DOREN ROBBINS has published nine collections of poetry, most recently *Amnesty Muse* (Lost Horse Press 2011). His work has appeared in *The American Poetry Review*, *Indiana Review*, *Hayden's Ferry Review*, *New Letters*, *North Dakota Quarterly*, and many other journals. He teaches creative writing, composition, and literature at Foothill College.

BARBARA ROCKMAN's poems have appeared or are forthcoming in *Bellingham Review*, *CALYX*, *Cimarron Review*, *Nimrod*, and *Spoon River Poetry Review*. She has received the Southwest Writers Prize, the New Mexico Discovery Award, *The MacGuffin* Poet Hunt Prize and Baskerville Publishers' Prize. She is the author of the poetry collection *Sting and Nest*, which received the 2011 New Mexico Press Women Prize for Poetry.

JAMIE ROSS writes and paints on a mesa west of Taos, New Mexico, and spends much of his time in Mexico. His poetry has been published in numerous journals, including *Nimrod*, as well as *Best New Poets 2007*. His 2010 collection, *Vinland*, received the Intro Poetry Prize from Four Way Books.

TOMAŽ ŠALAMUN lives in Ljubljana, Slovenia. He taught Spring semester 2011 at Michener Center for Writers at The University of Texas. His recent books translated into English are *The Blue Tower* (Houghton Mifflin Harcourt 2011) and *On the Tracks of Wild Game* (Ugly Duckling Presse 2012). His *Soy realidad*, translated by Michael Thomas Taren, is forthcoming by Dalkey Archive Press in 2014.

VINCE SGAMBATI was a semifinalist in the *Nimrod* Literary Awards in 2012. His fiction has also appeared in *North American Review*, *Gertrude Press*, and *Off The Rocks* (New Town Writers, Chicago). His creative nonfiction has appeared in the anthology *Queer and Catholic* (Routledge) and the *Journal of GLBT Family Studies*.

LEE SHARKEY's newest poetry volume, *Calendars of Fire*, has recently been published by Tupelo Press. Her poems have appeared or are forthcoming in *Crazyhorse*, *Field*, *Kenyon Review*, *The Pinch*, *Prairie Schooner*, and *The Seattle Review*. She was the Maine Arts Commission's 2010 Fellow in Literary Arts and serves as co-editor of the *Beloit Poetry Journal*.

ALIMA SHERMAN was born with a book in her hand. Her specialty is psychoneuroimmunology. She currently lives with her husband and chocolate Lab by the Pacific Ocean. She has published three chapbooks and is working on a book of poems, *Sloping East*.

LYNN SHOEMAKER grew up in South Dakota near the Missouri River. For many years he worked as a human rights activist and a teacher. Though retired, he continues to struggle for the rights of the planet, and to write poetry. His latest publication is a chapbook entitled *A Catch in the Throat of Allah*.

JOHN OLIVER SIMON is a translator who has published more than 450 translations of contemporary Latin American poets. He is Artistic Director of Poetry Inside Out, an in-school literary translation program sponsored by the Center for the Art of Translation. He is the River of Words Teacher of the Year for 2013.

ANITA SKEEN is Professor in the Residential College in the Arts and Humanities at Michigan State University, where she is the director of the Center for Poetry. She is coordinator of the annual Creative Arts Festival and Fall Writing Festivals at Ghost Ranch in Abiquiu, New Mexico.

Never the Whole Story is her most recent collection of poems, with *The Unauthorized Audubon* forthcoming.

LILVIA SOTO was born in Mexico and lives in Tucson, Arizona. She holds a Ph.D. in Latin American Literature, has taught in several American universities, and writes in both English and Spanish. She has published poetry, short fiction, literary criticism, and literary translations in the U.S., Spain, Canada, Mexico, and other Latin American countries.

LIANNE SPIDEL's poems have appeared in *Poetry, Shenandoah,* and *Southern Poetry Review,* among other literary journals, and more recently in *Atlanta Review* and *The Bayou Journal.* Others are forthcoming in *Poem, Hubbub,* and *Cloudbank.* Her chapbook of art poems, *Chrome,* was published in 2006 by Finishing Line Press. She lives in Greenville, Ohio.

MATTHEW J. SPIRENG's book *What Focus Is* was published by Word Press in 2011. His book *Out of Body* won the 2004 Bluestem Poetry Award. He has written five chapbooks, *Clear Cut, Young Farmer, Encounters, Inspiration Point,* winner of the 2000 Bright Hill Press Poetry Chapbook Competition, and *Just This.*

KAZ SUSSMAN is a curmudgeon recently ensared by the full moon. He has been a carpenter and a disaster response worker, and lives in a home he has built in Oregon from abandoned poems. His work is available or forthcoming in *Caduceus Journal, Boston Literary Magazine, Kingpin, The Raven Chronicles,* and *San Pedro River Review,* among other publications.

MICHAEL THOMAS TAREN's poems have been published or are forthcoming in *HTMLGIANT, The Claudius App, Fence,* and *Bestoned.* He spent nine months in Slovenia on a Fulbright Scholarship (2010-2011). His manuscripts *Puberty* and *Where Is Michael* were finalists for the Fence Modern Poets Series in 2009 and 2010.

SUE ELLEN THOMPSON is the author of four books of poetry, the editor of *The Autumn House Anthology of Contemporary American Poetry,* and the recipient of the 2010 Maryland Author Award. She lives on Maryland's Eastern Shore and teaches at The Writer's Center in Bethesda and Annapolis. Her new manuscript, *They,* will be published in 2014.

ANITA VITACOLONNA earned her Master's degree in English from Fordham University. She lived and worked in Africa and Italy for twenty years, raising a family and teaching. Since her return to the U.S., she has studied under several poets at George Mason University. Her work has been anthologized in *It All Begins: Poems from Post-Liberation South Africa*, and has appeared in U.S. and international journals.

MARY LEE WALDRON grew up in Taunton, Massachusetts, summers on Cape Cod. Married at twenty-one, she and her husband raised nine children in the Somerset Hills area of New Jersey. She has fourteen grandchildren and one great-grandchild. She coordinates a critique group in Women Who Write, Inc., and does pre-publication manuscript preparation for poetry chapbooks.

RONALD WALLACE's most recent books are *For A Limited Time Only* and *Long for This World: New and Selected Poems*. He co-directs the creative writing program at the University of Wisconsin and serves as poetry editor for the University of Wisconsin Press's Brittingham and Pollak Prize Poetry Series.

CAROL WAS's appreciation of the natural world was shaped by childhood summers in West Virginia, fishing trips with her father, teaching, and working with special needs children. She is the Poetry Editor for *The MacGuffin*, and her work has appeared in *The Gettysburg Review*, *The Southern Review*, and *Connecticut Review*. She's an active member of Springfed Arts-Metro Detroit Writers.

JULIA WENDELL's most recent book of poems, *The Sorry Flowers*, appeared from Word Tech Press in 2009, and her memoir, *Finding My Distance: A Year in the Life of a Three-day Event Rider*, was published by Galileo Press the same year. She lives and works on a horse farm in northern Baltimore County with her husband, poet Barrett Warner, and is a competition three-day event rider.

MARK WILLIAMS retired from the real estate business in Evansville, Indiana, where he lives with his wife DeeGee. His writing has appeared in *The Hudson Review*, *Indiana Review*, *The Southern Review*, and *Open 24 Hours*. A poem will appear in *Rattle* this year.

FRANCINE WITTE's flash-fiction chapbook, *The Wind Twirls Everything*, was published by MuscleHead Press. She is the winner of the Thomas A. Wilhelmus Award in fiction from Ropewalk Press, and her chapbook, *Cold June* was published in 2010. Her poetry chapbook *First Rain* was published in 2009 by Pecan Grove Press. Her poetry chapbook *Only, Not Only* is forthcoming from Finishing Line Press.

JACK WOLFTEICH was a counselor and group facilitator. He was a semifinalist in the *Davoren Hanna* Poetry Competition 2003, and his poems have been published online in the *NOTES*. He has been a contributor to local anthologies and readings in Florida as well as a featured reader at the Artwell foundation in Torrington, Connecticut.

LEAH ZAZULYER's publications include two poetry chapbooks, *The World Is a Wedding*, 1993; *Round Trip Year*, 1992; a full length poetry book *Songs the Zazulya Sang*, 2007; and *Siberia*, 1991, a book of translation of Israel Emiot; plus selections in a variety of journals and magazines. She has received grants from the Constance Saltonstall Arts Foundation, The New York State Council on the Arts, and the John Howe Award.

SETH ZIMMERMAN is a mathematician and poet in Washington state. His translations of the later poems of Osip Mandelstam have appeared in many journals, including *Nimrod*, and his rhymed, dual-language version of *The Inferno of Dante Alighieri* is accessible on the web.

SABINE BARNARD, AWS, NWS, is a signature member of the American and National watercolor societies and exhibits in Tulsa at M.A. Doran gallery. She is a freelance artist, illustrator, and art instructor. Her work is published in various art books and appears in corporate and private collectors in the U.S. and Europe.

ELEANOR LEONNE BENNETT is a sixteen-year-old internationally award-winning photographer and artist from the United Kingdom. Her photography has been on the covers of books and magazines in the United States and Canada. Her photo on page 187 first appeared on her etsy page, vintageandantiques12.etsy.com.

CONNIE BRYSON'S oil paintings have been displayed in Los Angeles and in national galleries, buildings, restaurants and spas. Her work is being published by Winn Devon Art Group and can be seen throughout the United States and the world. She is represented by Joseph Gierek Fine Art in Tulsa, Oklahoma.

KIM BULTMAN is a writer, musician, and photographer from Eufaula, Oklahoma, by way of Minnesota, whose formal education includes reading the directions and trucking across America. When she's not playing the piano or wandering the shores of Lake Eufaula, she can be found in the kitchen, cooking up adventures for her blog, www.alittlelunch.com.

TODD CAMP is an artist represented in Tulsa by Joseph Gierek Fine Art.

GEOFFREY BENJAMIN CHEW is an artist who lives in Haskell, Oklahoma.

GLENN HERBERT DAVIS was the recipient of a Oklahoma Visual Arts Fellowship in 2006. His work has been exhibited and published nationally. His solo work, "image of one," was exhibited at Berry College.

OTTO DUECKER has been exploring Realism for over thirty years. His work has been exhibited in New York, Illinois, California, New Mexico, and Oklahoma, and is featured in many collections. He graduated from Oklahoma State University. He is represented in Tulsa by M. A. Doran Gallery.

REGHINA GUNZUREVSCAIA was born in Moldova in the Soviet Republic. After the breakup and dissolution of the Soviet Union, she moved to Bulgaria with her family when she was fifteen. She has studied art and Greek language and has earned a degree in Mass Communication from Panteios University in Athens. She currently works for The Hellenic Foundation for the

Preservation of History and Culture, a foundation which seeks to preserve the significance of important Hellenic achievement.

STEVE LAUTERMILCH has traveled in the far west as a poet and photographer, exploring the sites and landscapes of the first peoples. *Rim*, a chapbook, won the 2010 Sow's Ear Press Award and received Honorable Mention in the 2012 Brockman-Campbell Awards from the North Carolina Poetry Society. New work appears in *The Comstock Review*, *Off the Coast*, and *String Poet*.

RON POKRASSO is an artist represented in Tulsa by Joseph Gierek Fine Art.

LESLIE PORRECA is a public defender, poet, and photographer. She lives, works, and plays in Venice, California.

CHICO SEAY has been an art photographer in Oklahoma since 1992. His work has been shown in numerous group and one- and two-man shows across the country and internationally. His work is represented in galleries in Dallas and Portland. He lives in Mannford, Oklahoma.

JAMES ANDREW SMITH attended the Kansas City Art Institute. He worked for ten years as a designer before formally beginning his art career in 2001. His work is exhibited in Tulsa through Joseph Gierek Gallery.

KELLEY VANDIVER was born in Daytona, Florida, grew up in Buffalo, New York, began his career as a painter in Tulsa, Oklahoma, and now lives and paints in San Miguel de Allende, Mexico. He is represented in Tulsa by Joseph Gierek Fine Art.

MARK WEISS, an ophthalmologist in Tulsa, Oklahoma, is an award-winning photographer.

HAWAI'I PACIFIC REVIEW

An annual literary magazine publishing
outstanding poetry, fiction, and personal essays
by authors from Hawai'i, the mainland,
and around the world.

Individual subscriptions
$8.95 for current issue • $16.00 for two issues
$22.00 for three issues

Institutional subscriptions
$10.00 for current issue • $18.00 for two issues
$25.00 for three issues

Best of the Decade, 1986-1996 (double issue)
$10.00

Best of the Decade, 1997-2007 (double issue)
$10.00

All other back issues
$5.00

Manuscripts accepted
September 1 through December 31

Patrice Wilson, Ph.D., Editor
Hawai'i Pacific Review
Hawai'i Pacific University
1060 Bishop Street, LB7
Honolulu, Hawai'i 96813
E-mail: hpreview@hpu.edu
Submissions: hprsubmissions@hpu.edu
Website: www.hpu.edu/hpr

Lasting Matters

WRITERS 57 AND OVER . . .